metaphor -
2 unlike objects
w/o like or as

simili — w/ like or as

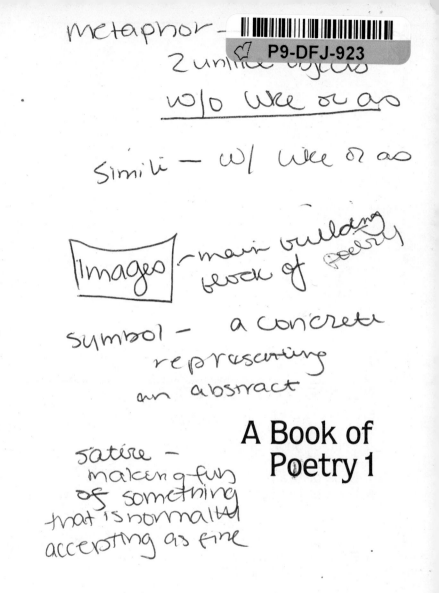

Images — main building
block of poetry

symbol — a concrete
representing
an abstract

satire —
making fun
of something
that is normally
accepting as fine

**A Book of
Poetry 1**

PERSPECTIVES IN LITERATURE

SECOND EDITION

A Book of Short Stories 1
A Book of Poetry 1
A Book of Drama 1
A Book of Nonfiction 1

A Book of Short Stories 2
A Book of Poetry 2
A Book of Drama 2
A Book of Nonfiction 2

SECOND EDITION

A BOOK OF POETRY 1

Secondary English Staff
Harcourt Brace Jovanovich, Publishers

HARCOURT BRACE JOVANOVICH, PUBLISHERS

Orlando New York Chicago San Diego Atlanta Dallas

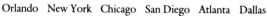

For permission to reprint copyrighted material, grateful acknowledgement is made to the following sources:

Margaret Walker Alexander: "Iowa Farmer" and "Childhood" from *For My People* by Margaret Walker, Yale University Press, 1942.

Brandt & Brandt Literary Agents, Inc.: "The Ballad of Marco Polo" by Stephen Vincent Benét, copyright 1939 by The Atlantic Monthly Company.

Sterling A. Brown: "After Winter" by permission of Sterling A. Brown.

John Ciardi: "One Morning" from *Person To Person* by John Ciardi. Copyright © 1964 by Rutgers University Press.

Molly Malone Cook Literary Agency, Inc. and Houghton Mifflin Company: "Letter From Home" from *No Voyage and Other Poems* by Mary Oliver. Copyright © 1965 by Mary Oliver.

R.P. Dickey: "Shazam" by R.P. Dickey, which originally appeared in *Concise Dictionary of Lead River, Mo.*, © 1972 by R.P. Dickey.

Doubleday & Company, Inc.: "The Sloth" copyright 1950 by Theodore Roethke. "The Meadow Mouse" copyright © 1963 by Beatrice Roethke as Administratrix for the Estate of Theodore Roethke. Both poems are from *The Collected Poems of Theodore Roethke*. Excerpts from *The Odyssey*, translated by Robert Fitzgerald. Copyright © 1961 by Robert Fitzgerald.

Norma Millay Ellis: "This door You Might Not Open" and "First Fig" from *Collected Poems* by Edna St. Vincent Millay, Harper & Row. Copyright 1917, 1922, 1945, 1950 by Edna St. Vincent Millay and Norma Millay Ellis.

Farrar, Straus and Giroux, Inc.: "The Fish" from *Elizabeth Bishop: The Complete Poems* by Elizabeth Bishop. Copyright © 1940, 1969 by Elizabeth Bishop. "Musician" from *The Blue Estuaries* by Louise Bogan. Copyright © 1937, 1968 by Louise Bogan. Copyright renewed © 1965 by Louise Bogan.

Harcourt Brace Jovanovich, Inc.: "Limited" from *Chicago Poems* by Carl Sandburg, copyright 1916 by Holt, Rinehart and Winston, Inc.; copyright 1944 by Carl Sandburg. "Jazz Fantasia" from *Smoke and Steel* by Carl Sandburg, copyright 1920 by Harcourt Brace Jovanovich, Inc., renewed 1948 by Carl Sandburg. "Boy at the Window" from *Things of This World* by Richard Wilbur. © 1952 by the New Yorker Magazine, Inc. "Dream-

Contributor: Flora Wallis Foss
Kishwaukee Junior College, Malta, Illinois
Formerly of the Geneva, Illinois Public School System

Critical reader: L. Harlan Ford, Ed.D.
President of American Technological University, Killeen, Texas
Former Deputy Commissioner of Education for the State of Texas

Cover photo: © Rocky Weldon/Leo de Wys

Production: LMD Service for Publishers

CONTENTS

A Book of
Poetry 1

INTRODUCTION

Near the Old North Bridge in Concord, Massachusetts, is a statue of a man dressed in militia coat, leggings, and a tricornered hat. In one hand he holds a musket. Beside him is his plow. This statue, called "The Minute Man," is a memorial to the farmers who began the Revolutionary War when they gathered at the bridge on April 19, 1775, and turned back British soldiers marching from Lexington.

On the base of the monument is the following inscription:

> By the rude bridge that arched the flood,
> Their flag to April's breeze unfurled,
> Here once the embattled farmers stood,
> And fired the shot heard round the world.

These words, the opening stanza of a sixteen-line poem, "Concord Hymn," were read by their author, the American poet-philosopher Ralph Waldo Emerson, on Independence Day in 1837 at the dedication of the monument.

If a prose statement instead of a poem had been written to commemorate the Minute Men, the following lines might have appeared on the monument:

> This statue is a tribute to the brave, freedom-loving farmers, who, on April 19, 1775, fought the first battle of the American Revolution and affected the lives of people everywhere.

The sentence contains more information than the poem does, but it appears flat by comparison. Why? One reason is that the poem presents a description of the event: the rough-hewn ("rude"), arched bridge over the rushing river ("the flood"), the flag unfurling in the spring breeze, and the farmers firing the first shots. The scene comes alive because of the poet's use of *images,* words or phrases which suggest what we can know through our senses of sight, hearing, touch, taste, or smell.

Denotation and Connotation

In making images, the poet selects words that can affect us strongly. They affect us not only with their *denotations,* or dictionary meanings, but also with their *connotations,* the impressions the words call to mind. For example, why did Emerson choose the word *rude* to describe the bridge?

Of the several meanings we find for *rude* in the dictionary, we would select the one which applies to things: "being marked by a rough, plain, or unfinished condition." If we were to define *rude bridge* denotatively, therefore, we would say "a bridge made of unfinished lumber."

The word *rude,* however, was probably chosen by Emerson because its connotations apply here as well as its denotations. The word suggests a rural area where people were in some ways unrefined, or untrained in the genteel arts. The "rude bridge" was built solely for practical reasons; there was no time or energy wasted on finishing it off or trying to make it beautiful. "Rude bridge" prepares us for "embattled farmers," men who worked with their hands and were not trained to fight. These men were essentially builders and cultivators, not destroyers.

All words have denotative meanings, and many have connotative meanings as well. Often we respond to the connotations of words without being aware that we are doing so. Reading a poem is a much richer experience, however, for the person who thinks about the connotations of the poet's words.

Both the prose writer and the poet use words that bring to mind no more than the dictionary definition, as well as words that are rich in connotations. The poet, however, generally uses more connotative words than the prose writer. He or she uses fewer words than the prose writer, but tries to say more with each word. To most poets, a completely denotative word is like a stone: it may be useful, but it has no life. Connotative words, however, are like stones thrown into water: the first stone creates ripples, movement; the second creates ripples that interact with the first; and so on. Words come alive, and the objects that the poet is describing, the ideas and emotions with which he or she is concerned, come alive.

Figures of Speech

Connotative words are often arranged in phrases which we call *figures of speech*. A figure of speech generally suggests a meaning by comparison. "His voice sounds like a foghorn" is a figure of speech in which the sound of a man's voice is compared to the sound of a foghorn. A figure of speech in which there is an indirect comparison by means of the words *like* or *as* is called a *simile*. A figure of speech in which there is a direct comparison without *like* or *as* is called a *metaphor*. "She sees the world through rose-colored glasses" is a metaphor in which an optimistic outlook is compared to the use of glasses which give everything a rosy glow. "The snow blanketed the town" is a metaphor in which a verb (blanketed) is used to compare the effect of the snow to that of a blanket.

There are other figures of speech such as *personification,* in which the writer attributes human qualities to animals, inanimate objects, or ideas. However, simile and metaphor are the most frequently used figures of speech.

Other Elements of Poetry

Poems, however, are more than collections of highly connotative words and figures of speech. The words of a poem are contained by a form, often distinguished from prose passages by the presence of *rhyme* and *rhythm* patterns.

Rhyme

Rhyme occurs when the same sound is repeated in two words placed close to each other. For example, the following lines from the poem "Aladdin" by James Russell Lowell contain two rhymes:

> When I was a beggarly boy
> And lived in a cellar damp,
> I had not a friend nor a toy,
> But I had Aladdin's lamp.

In these lines, *boy* rhymes with *toy,* and *damp* with *lamp.* That is, the sounds /oy/ and /amp/ each appear twice. (In discussing rhyme, we often refer to the rhyming sounds by italicized letters. The first rhyme is indicated by *a*, the second by *b*, and so on. The rhyme pattern or scheme of these four lines is therefore *abab*.)

Why did the poet want his lines to rhyme? Why did he reverse the normal order of *damp cellar* (line 2) to make a rhyme? One reason is that rhyme, like most of the techniques the poet uses, has a special sound effect: it is pleasing to the ear. Songwriters have known this for centuries. If you repeat the words of most songs, old or new, you will see that the lyrics generally make up rhymed verses.

Rhythm and Meter

Poetry is close to music in many ways. Some poems were originally meant to be sung. Poets, like composers of music, usually pay a great deal of attention to rhythm, the underlying beat of a poem or a musical composition. In poetry as well as music, the rhythm is sometimes so strong that you can tap your foot to it.

Rhythm is the result of a contrast between accented or stressed syllables and unaccented or unstressed syllables. A stressed syllable is one which the speaker emphasizes. For example, in the word *beggarly,* the syllable *beg* is stressed and the syllables *gar* and *ly* are unstressed. (The word is therefore pronounced BEG•gar•ly.) Poets do not always use the same rhythm throughout a poem, but usually there is a fairly regular, organized rhythmic pattern. This rhythmic pattern is called *meter.* Meter is a second quality which often distinguishes poetry from prose.

The meter of a poem is found by counting, or *scanning,* the number and placement of stressed and unstressed syllables in a line of poetry. The syllables are scanned in groups called *feet.* Each *foot* has at least one stressed syllable; it usually has one or two unstressed syllables. The line, Their FLAG/to A/pril's BREEZE/unFURLED, contains four feet, or four groups, each of which contains one unstressed and one stressed syllable, in that order. Each foot of this type is called an *iamb,* and the meter of the line is called *iambic.* Iambic meter is the most common meter in poetry written in English.

Another common meter is *trochaic* (trō•kā′ik), which is the reverse of iambic. In trochaic meter, a stressed syllable is followed by an unstressed syllable, as in the following line from Henry Wadsworth Longfellow's "Hiawatha": DARK be/HIND it/

ROSE the/FORest. Each foot in trochaic meter is called a *trochee*.

Sometimes the poet chooses a particular meter and uses it more or less strictly to appeal to our sense of rhythm. (However, he or she usually varies the meter somewhat to avoid a boring singsong effect.) Often he or she tries to communicate some of the meaning through the choice of meter or through changes in meter within the poem.

Rhythm or meter may be used to communicate a mood, an idea, or an effect. The poem may change the normal order of words so that certain words are stressed by the metric pattern. Rhythm may appeal to the same instincts within us that we respond to with music. Rhythm, like imagery, appeals to the senses.

The Types of Poetry

Poetry may be divided into three major types: (1) narrative, (2) lyric, and (3) dramatic. Although there are similar characteristics in all three types, each category has distinctive features.

Narrative poems narrate; that is, they tell a story. The story may be long and complicated, with many characters involved in numerous events; or it may be brief, with one character in conflict with another or with a situation. Narrative poems are similar to short stories in that they have a setting, plot, and characters, and usually have dialogue.

Lyric poems are generally short poems which communicate the emotional response of a speaker to a person, place, object, or idea. Among the common subjects of lyric poems are love and nature.

Dramatic poems usually reveal more about the speakers' personality than do lyrics or narratives. In a dramatic poem, the speakers talk to each other, revealing conflicts or problems that disturb them. As in narrative poetry, they may tell a story, but the main emphasis is on their reaction to the events rather than on the events themselves.

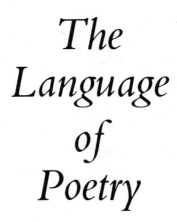

The
Language
of
Poetry

IMAGE, SIMILE, METAPHOR

An experience which left a deep impression makes the poet want to re-create the effect of the experience in a poem. To accomplish this the poem must use language that involves the senses, charging them with the emotions of that moment. Images are the "word pictures" that allow us to see, hear, feel, taste, even smell the objects and motions that the poet wants us to sense. Just as the words making up an image must awaken the senses, so they must also be able to call up or suggest meanings beyond the obvious. The *connotations* or associations of some of the words of a poem help communicate the mood or emotions of the moment. Look, for example, at Theodore Roethke's "The Meadow Mouse" (p. 33). He pictures the animal he holds in his palm as

A little quaker, the whole body of him trembling,
His absurd whiskers sticking out like a cartoon-mouse,
His feet like small leaves . . .

The image in the first line tells us that the mouse is shaking all over. But by choosing the word "trembling" Roethke has relied on our associations of fear and discomfort with trembling to make us sense the mouse's misery and terror. By calling the mouse "a little quaker," he makes us think not only of the denotation of "quake" (shake) but also of the religious sect of Quakers, or Society of Friends. Indirectly, the mouse is associated with those who are peace-loving and prayerful. The association makes us appreciate the mouse's wish to be left alone and its total helplessness before the speaker.

In the lines above, Roethke has also used *similes* (see the discussion of figures of speech in the Introduction, p. 3), comparisons using the words *like* or *as,* to build on the simple image with which he begins. We aren't really being asked to think of the mouse's feet as small leaves, although they do appear like them in some ways. However, we know leaves are frail and at the mercy of the elements, and the comparison makes us associate this vulnerability with the mouse. When the "absurd whiskers" make the poet think of a cartoon-mouse, we don't think of the creature as unreal, but the association makes us smile and reminds us that this is a real creature whose life depends on the person now holding it. As a result, we feel even more sympathy for the mouse than if the poet had taken it for granted that we felt the aliveness of the creature.

A second type of figure of speech often used by poets is the *metaphor* (see the introductory discussion, p. 3), a direct comparison which does not use *like* or *as*. In "Mother to Son" Langston Hughes compares life to a difficult stairway that must be climbed:

> Life for me ain't been no crystal stair.
> It's had tacks in it,
> And splinters,
> And boards torn up . . .

Often image or simile and metaphor are used to reinforce and strengthen one another. In these lines we find the comparison made more striking by the images of unpleasant, discouraging obstacles that must be faced as one "climbs the stair," or goes through life.

WILLIAM (EDGAR) STAFFORD
(born 1914)

William Stafford was born and educated in Kansas, and received a B.A. and an M.A. from the University of Kansas and a Ph.D. from the University of Iowa. The land in which he grew up was an important shaping influence on Stafford, who places high value on the natural world. He also places high value on human life.

The reader of Stafford's poems gets a strong sense of his closeness to the land and his concern over our destruction of so much of nature. Stafford does not, however, set himself up as a critic of "man the polluter"; instead, he balances his love for the land and its creatures with an understanding that he is a human being, part of the civilized world with its technology and enormous requirements. He does not accuse people of thoughtless destruction or suggest easy solutions that will allow human beings and their civilization to exist in harmony with nature. Rather, Stafford probes with a calm, gentle, honest voice to make himself and the reader more "aware of what being alive means." * This awareness does not always make the reader feel happy and peaceful, but it offers an enriched, enlarged view of life.

This important contemporary poet has published many books and was given the National Book Award in 1963. His poems are widely read by people of all ages. This must please Stafford, because it is for this end that he wants to write poems that "speak . . . the language of everyday." * As you will find in "Listening," the language of his poem is simple and straightforward. The poem shows, however, that everyday occurrences can be moving, important, and more complex than they seem on first consideration.

* Taken from Stafford's statement in *The Distinctive Voice: Twentieth Century American Poetry,* ed. William Martz (Glenview, Ill.: Scott Foresman, 1966).

Listening

My father could hear a little animal step,
or a moth in the dark against the screen,
and every far sound called the listening out
into places where the rest of us had never been.

5   More spoke to him from the soft wild night
than came to our porch for us on the wind;
we would watch him look up and his face go keen
till the walls of the world flared, widened.

My father heard so much that we still stand
10   inviting the quiet by turning the face,
waiting for a time when something in the night
will touch us too from that other place.

Meaning and Method

1. In the first stanza, what image does the speaker use to make us feel the keenness and power of the father's listening? Why would the speaker admire the father's ability to hear things from "places where the rest of us had never been"?
2. In lines 7–8, a simple image leads into a metaphor which stretches beyond the room where the family sat. What is the image? What comparison does the metaphor make? In what sense do you think the speaker means the world has walls? What has made them flare and widen? What is there about the setting the speaker is remembering that makes this comparison seem appropriate?
3. The poem tells us that the wild night sounds can "speak" to us (line 5) and "touch" us (line 12), that they "call the listening out" (line 3) instead of sending in noises for the ears (as we usually think of listening). Is this a quality of listening that is different from listening only with the ears? What kind of person do the details suggest would be able to listen as the father did?

Composition

The speaker in "Listening" felt his world opened up and enlivened by the "voice" and "touch" of natural sounds. Think of some experience which made the "walls" of your world flare and widen. Write a description of the experience, and explain how you felt your understanding or personality grow as a result.

JOHN CIARDI*
(born 1916)

The number of John Ciardi's achievements reveals the vitality and fertility of his mind as well as a willingness to try new things. Besides having written many volumes of poetry, he has written numerous books (both prose and poetry) for children, has translated the major works of Dante, and has edited several important critical works. The number of prizes and honorary degrees awarded Ciardi in recognition of his poetic achievement is also impressive.

Ciardi's zest for life and his ability to turn his energy into achievement were apparent early in his life. Born and educated in Massachusetts, he was graduated *magna cum laude* from Tufts College in 1938. The next year, he won the Hopwood Award for Poetry while earning his M.A. at the University of Michigan.

If it is part of Ciardi's nature as a poet to be prolific and constantly to attempt new things, it is also characteristic of him to inject a strong personal quality into his work. Some have criticized his poetry for this quality; others see it as a natural and effective celebration of his "delight in the world, the interest which his own life affords him." Ciardi does more than create a self-portrait by giving a sense of his individuality in his poems. In the best ones, the personal quality expresses a universality which links all people to the writer. In Ciardi's own words, the poem then gives the reader "one of the voices of his humanity . . . quickened to itself."†

* **Ciardi** (chär′dē).
† Both quotations taken from *Contemporary Poets,* ed. James Vinson (London: St. James Press, 1975), p. 246.

One Morning

I remember my littlest one in a field
running so hard at the morning in him
he kicked the heads off daisies. Oh, wild
and windy and spilling over the brim
5   of his sun-up juices he ran
in the dew of himself. My son.

And the white flower heads
shot like sparks where his knees
pumped, and his hot-shod
10   feet took off from time, as who knows
when ever again a running morning will be
so light-struck, flower-sparked-full between him and me.

Meaning and Method

1. Youngsters do things intensely; they work hard even at their play. With what images does the speaker show this intensity in the boy's running?
2. The father feels his young son's exuberance and zest for living as he watches him run through the field. He calls this spirit "the morning in him." What words or phrases does he use in the first stanza to extend the comparison? In what ways is youth like morning?
3. With the phrases "feet took off from time" (line 10) and "running morning" (line 11) the father emphasizes the idea that time passes—a boy grows up and morning becomes midday. But this scene is carved out of time, unforgettable because its details are seen sharply and freshly, and related to the love the father feels for his son's new life. For example, how does the father's impression of the daisies seem unusual and memorable? How does he relate the flowers to his feelings for his son in the last line?

Compare and Contrast

In "Listening" a son remembers a special strength he felt in his father; in "One Morning" a father captures a memory of some power in his son. How is nature used to reveal this power in each poem? What time of day is important in each? Are the strengths of the people each speaker remembers similar or different? Explain.

WILLIAM BUTLER YEATS*
(1865–1939)

The poems of William Butler Yeats, one of the greatest poets of the twentieth century, were strongly affected by his love and concern for his native Ireland. This attachment was no doubt strengthened by the fact that he lived through a difficult period of Irish revolt and final independence from Great Britain. Although Yeats's poems speak to people of all countries, a great many of them deal with Ireland and its people. They range in subject matter from legends of Irish heroes (both historic and supernatural) to keen observations of everyday Irish men and women, from the countryside where he grew up to the revolution and civil war that tore his country.

Yeats was determined to be a great poet from an early age, and thought continually about the type of poetry he wanted to write. As a young man, he wrote poems that are melodious and rich in images and figurative language. Yeats, however, did not continue to write this type of poetry. Slowly, his view of life and poetry changed, and his poems reflected these changes. As he grew older, his aim in writing verse was to be "as cold and passionate as the dawn." Most of his later poems have a conciseness, concreteness, and force which are largely absent from his early poems. It was primarily for these qualities that he was awarded the Nobel Prize for literature in 1923.

In 1889 Yeats fell in love with the beautiful Maud Gonne who drew him into the Irish National movement, about which Yeats had strong doubts. Maud Gonne's marriage to John MacBride, in 1903, marked an important change in Yeats's life. Disappointed in love, he resolved to make great poetry out of his experience, seeking perfection in his work rather than in his life.

In 1917 Yeats married the English woman Georgie Hyde-Lee, and his two children were born in 1919 and 1921. He became a senator in the Irish Free State, founded in 1921. By the time of his death, Yeats had become the leading poet of his age, who had taught "the free man how to praise," as W. H. Auden wrote of him in his great elegiac poem, "In Memory of W. B. Yeats (D. Jan. 1939)."

* **Yeats** (yāts).

The Lake Isle of Innisfree*

I will arise and go now, and go to Innisfree,
And a small cabin build there, of clay and wattles°
    made:
Nine bean-rows will I have there, a hive for
    the honeybee,
        And live alone in the bee-loud glade.

5   And I shall have some peace there, for peace comes
        dropping slow,
    Dropping from the veils of the morning to where
        the cricket sings;
    There midnight's all a glimmer, and noon a purple glow,
        And evening full of the linnet's° wings.

    I will arise and go now, for always night and day
10   I hear lake water lapping with low sounds by the shore;
    While I stand on the roadway, or on the pavements gray,
        I hear it in the deep heart's core.

* **Innisfree:** an island near Sligo, which Yeats visited as a child. **2. wattles:** twigs and flexible rods woven together. **8. linnet:** a songbird.

Meaning and Method

1. What does the speaker hope to find at Innisfree? Why can he not find this quality in his present surroundings? Why is it appropriate that Innisfree is an island?
2. Yeats uses images which appeal strongly to the senses of hearing (e.g., "live alone in the bee-loud glade") and sight (e.g., "midnight's all a glimmer"). Point out other images evoking sights and sounds. What do these images communicate about the atmosphere of Innisfree? Is it fast-moving? slow? dreamlike? businesslike? Are its sounds soothing or irritating?
3. Yeats's use of long lines and repetition of /l/ and /s/ sounds also help create the mood of the poem. Read it aloud; then tell how you think these techniques help us sense the atmosphere of the island.

Composition

Describe a place which you once enjoyed and to which you would like to return. Try, like Yeats, to use specific details which show why you are attracted to this place.

Compare and Contrast

In both "Listening" and "The Lake Isle of Innisfree" the speaker is remembering something precious from childhood. How do the places and actions (or stillness) each speaker remembers seem alike? seem different? What effect does the memory have on each speaker?

MARIANNE MOORE
(1887–1972)

Before the Brooklyn Dodgers were transformed into the Los Angeles Dodgers, they probably had no greater fan than an erudite poet who lived in Brooklyn and wore gay, elaborate hats. In verse as well as in person, Marianne Moore, the poet, cheered the Dodgers. "A neat bunt, please; a cloud breaker, a drive . . . ," she once implored them in a poem written during a World Series.

Her poems are experimental and complex in form, yet her philosophy of life is based on conventional and basically simple values. She admires such virtues as fortitude, self-reliance, and endurance, and believes, as she once said, "that the unselfish behavior of individual to individual is the basis of world peace." Although her work is deeply rooted in other people's writings, the individuality of her poems is their most striking characteristic. She builds many of her poems around quotations from surprisingly varied sources, such as Leo Tolstoy's diary, the regulations of the Department of the Interior, and advertisements found in newspapers.

Marianne Moore was born in St. Louis, Missouri, and educated at a private school in Carlisle, Pennsylvania. She attended Bryn Mawr College, and after graduation returned to Carlisle to study at the Carlisle Commercial School. From 1911 through 1915, she taught commercial subjects at the Indian School in Carlisle.

In the 1920's after she had moved to New York, she worked as a librarian at the New York Public Library, and then spent several years as the editor of *Dial,* one of the most influential and forward-looking literary magazines of the period.

Miss Moore's poems have had a special attraction for other poets, who admire her technical mastery, vivid and original images, and subtlety of thought and expression. The value of her verse was acknowledged in 1951 when her *Collected Poems* was awarded the Pulitzer Prize for poetry.

Silence

My father used to say,
"Superior people never make long visits,
have to be shown Longfellow's grave
or the glass flowers at Harvard.
5 Self-reliant like the cat—
that takes its prey to privacy,
the mouse's limp tail hanging like a shoelace from its
mouth—
they sometimes enjoy solitude,
and can be robbed of speech
10 by speech which has delighted them.
The deepest feeling always shows itself in silence;
not in silence, but restraint."
Nor was he insincere in saying, "Make my house
your inn."
Inns are not residences.

Meaning and Method

1. According to the father in this poem, which of the following
are characteristics of "superior people": **a.** self-reliance; **b.** silence; **c.** restraint; **d.** concern for and responsiveness to other
people; **e.** something else?
2. Explain the last two lines. How does the thought expressed in
these lines follow from the theory of "superior people" expressed by the father in the first twelve lines, especially in line 2?

Composition

To what places in your town or city would you take a visitor
who had only one day to spend with you? Why would you choose
these places? Are there places you would deliberately avoid? If so,
why? Do you think a town or city is best shown by taking your
visitors to specific places, or by letting them wander at will? Include your answers to these questions in a composition combining
description and explanation.

TED KOOSER
(born 1939)

Born in Ames, Iowa, Ted Kooser graduated from Iowa State University in 1962. After a year of graduate study at the University of Nebraska, he went to work at a job (which he still holds), that of insurance underwriter. If the unlikely occupation does not hint at Kooser's artistic inclinations, other of his activities do. For eight years he edited and published a literary magazine, *The New Salt Creek Reader*. In addition to writing his own poems, he paints, and also runs a small press in Lincoln, Nebraska.

Although the geographic boundaries of his world are limited to the Midwest, Kooser has found in that landscape a rich world for poetic expression. In theme and subject his poems concentrate on familiar Midwestern objects and scenes. Out of his observations of the landscape, he creates poems that do much more than describe surface particulars. They capture and sharply focus moments in the lives of the people who inhabit this empty, flat country—and do so simply, with refreshingly honest, clear language. As "Abandoned Farmhouse" illustrates, a Kooser poem which at first appears to be about a farm building or animals actually tells a story of vulnerable people and unyielding land balanced against each other.

Kooser's first book, *Official Entry Blank,* was published in 1969. Between 1971 and 1978 seven more books of his poems appeared. In 1976 he was awarded a fellowship from the National Endowment for the Arts. This rapid progress in his poetic career reflects the enthusiasm with which his work has been read, as does the praise of some critics, who have cited his "special gifts of honest, lucid, and courageous perception" and even called him "the best young poet in this country."

Abandoned Farmhouse

He was a big man, says the size of his shoes
on a pile of broken dishes by the house;
a tall man too, says the length of the bed
in an upstairs room; and a good, God-fearing man,
5 says the Bible with a broken back
on the floor below a window, bright with sun;
but not a man for farming, say the fields
cluttered with boulders and a leaky barn.

A woman lived with him, says the bedroom wall
10 papered with lilacs and the kitchen shelves
covered with oilcloth, and they had a child
says the sandbox made from a tractor tire.
Money was scarce, say the jars of plum preserves
and canned tomatoes sealed in the cellar-hole,
15 and the winters cold, say the rags in the window-frames.
It was lonely here, says the narrow country road.

Something went wrong, says the empty house
in the weed-choked yard. Stones in the fields
say he was not a farmer; the still-sealed jars
20 in the cellar say she left in a nervous haste.
And the child? Its toys are strewn in the yard
like branches after a storm—a rubber cow,
a rusty tractor and a broken plow,
a doll in overalls. Something went wrong, they say.

Meaning and Method

1. Although the family has gone, how are we made to picture the
man, woman and child? In your answer, point out images that
show the personality and daily activities of each. For example,
in lines 4–6, how might the picture of the Bible with a broken
back make us realize that the man valued religion? What indication might there be that he loved to look out over the land
and feel the sun on his face?

2. What images make the hardships of their lives clear? In each image you point out, explain what associations the words call up to help build the feeling of poverty or loneliness.

3. What images show us that "something went wrong" (line 17)? For each detail, tell what connotations of the words make us think that trouble made them leave hastily.

Composition

Write a brief sketch or a poem in which the objects of a place explain the personality and give a sense of the daily routine of someone who lives there. A line from such a sketch might read like this: "She was a tidy, orderly woman, say the pots and pans, shining from their neat hanging rows on the kitchen wall."

KARL SHAPIRO
(born 1913)

Karl Shapiro was so interested in becoming a poet that he left the University of Virginia in 1933, after one year of study, to devote his time to reading and writing poetry. When his work was ignored, he returned to college—this time to Johns Hopkins University in Baltimore, his birthplace—only to have his college career interrupted by financial troubles and World War II.

The poems Shapiro wrote as a soldier stationed in the Pacific were enthusiastically received, unlike his first ones. By the end of the war, three highly successful books had been published in the U.S. Each was reprinted several times, and the second one, *V-Letter,* was awarded a Pulitzer Prize in 1945.

Shapiro's first two wartime volumes made vivid reading because of what one critic called his "interest in his immediate surroundings," and because of his ironic but deeply concerned approach to modern life. The poems in those volumes, and some of his later poems, were admired for "the accuracy and sensitivity of his observation," and for what the poet Babette Deutsch called the "prominence of feeling."

In his third wartime book, *Essay On Rime,* Shapiro used a very different approach. This book severely criticized modern poetry, which Shapiro felt was "in decline" because it did not deal with the problems which confront individuals in the modern world. In subsequent volumes of poetry and criticism, he has continued to discuss what he feels are the problems and failures of poets and poetry in the modern age.

Manhole Covers

The beauty of manhole covers—what of that?
Like medals struck by a great savage khan,
Like Mayan calendar stones,° unliftable, indecipherable,

3. **Mayan calendar stones:** The Mayans, a Central American Indian tribe, had an advanced civilization before the Europeans arrived. Among the signs of civilization was the development of a calendar which was carved on enormous stones.

Not like old electrum,° chased and scored,°
5   Mottoed and sculptured to a turn,
But notched and whelked and pocked and smashed
With the great company names:
Gentle Bethlehem, smiling United States.
This rustproof artifact° of my street,
10   Long after roads are melted away, will lie
Sidewise in the grave of the iron-old world,
Bitten at the edges,
Strong with its cryptic American,
Its dated beauty.

4. **electrum:** a gold-silver alloy used in making coins; **chased and scored:** When coins are chased, they are stamped and embossed; when they are scored, they are given a grooved edge around the rim. 9. **artifact:** anything made by human labor; usually refers to something found after a civilization has vanished.

Meaning and Method

1. Find phrases in the poem to show that the speaker thinks the manhole covers are beautiful because of their weight, their deep, rough indentations, and the power of the companies that made them.
2. Does the comparison of manhole covers to "medals struck by a great savage khan" (line 2) and to "Mayan calendar stones" (line 3) indicate that the poet thinks that American civilization, of which the manhole covers are a symbol, is extremely powerful? that it, like these other civilizations, will inevitably pass away? What words or phrases in lines 13–14 might be used to equate American civilization with Mayan civilization?

Composition

Begin your composition with Shapiro's first line, but substitute for "manhole covers" an object which most people would think of as useful but not beautiful. For example, you can choose to describe a screwdriver, a wrench, a shopping cart, a toothbrush, a refrigerator, or a can-opener. Use words which will indicate the way the object looks and feels to you.

SYLVIA PLATH
(1932–1963)

Sylvia Plath was born in Boston. She attended Smith College and while there spent one summer as a guest editor at *Mademoiselle*. During her junior year she suffered a nervous breakdown. However she returned to graduate with high honors and went on to spend two years at Cambridge University in England as a Fulbright scholar. In 1956 she married the English poet Ted Hughes; they had a daughter and a son. In 1957–1958 she taught at Smith, returning to England in 1959.

Her first book, *The Colossus,* was published in 1960. It was the only volume of her poems to be published before her early death at the age of thirty. The three volumes that came after her death make it plain that the last years of her life were deeply troubled. Besides her poetry she wrote short stories, a play and an autobiographical novel about a prize-winning college writer who suffers a nervous collapse.

Like Robert Lowell, John Berryman, Anne Sexton and others, Sylvia Plath has been called a "confessional poet," because much of her writing deals with deep, personal experiences.

Blackberrying

Nobody in the lane, and nothing, nothing but
   blackberries,
Blackberries on either side, though on the right mainly,
A blackberry alley, going down in hooks, and a sea
Somewhere at the end of it, heaving. Blackberries
5   Big as the ball of my thumb, and dumb as eyes
Ebon in the hedges, fat
With blue-red juices. These they squander on my fingers.
I had not asked for such a blood sisterhood; they must
   love me.
They accommodate themselves to my milkbottle,
   flattening their sides.

10   Overhead go the choughs° in black, cacophonous° flocks—
      Bits of burnt paper wheeling in a blown sky.
      Theirs is the only voice, protesting, protesting.
      I do not think the sea will appear at all.
      The high, green meadows are glowing, as if lit
          from within.
15   I come to one bush of berries so ripe it is a bush of flies,
      Hanging their blue-green bellies and their wing panes
          in a Chinese screen.
      The honey-feast of the berries has stunned them; they
          believe in heaven.
      One more hook, and the berries and bushes end.

      The only thing to come now is the sea.
20   From between two hills a sudden wind funnels at me,
      Slapping its phantom laundry in my face.
      These hills are too green and sweet to have tasted salt.
      I follow the sheep path between them. A last hook
          brings me
      To the hills' northern face, and the face is orange rock
25   That looks out on nothing, nothing but a great space
      Of white and pewter lights, and a din like silversmiths
      Beating and beating at an intractable° metal.

      10. choughs (chŭf): a European bird like the crow;   **cacophonous:**
      harsh-sounding, raucous.   **27. intractable:** unmanageable, stubborn,
      resistant.

Meaning and Method

1. The figures of speech in this poem are mainly metaphors and
   similes. What is being identified with "Bits of burnt paper
   wheeling in a blown sky" (line 11) and "Slapping its phantom
   laundry in my face" (line 21)? Why are these metaphors appropriate? Explain the meaning of the simile introduced in the last
   two lines of the poem.
2. Why does the poet see the blackberries as "a bush of flies"?
   How are "their wing panes in a Chinese screen"?

LANGSTON HUGHES
(1902–1967)

A combination of talent, courage, and luck gave Hughes his start as a poet. Hughes, working as a busboy at a hotel in Washington, D.C., recognized the poet Vachel Lindsay, and left some poems beside his plate. The poems so impressed the older poet that he read them at a recital of poetry and introduced Hughes to people who could publish his poems in magazines.

Hughes's work soon began to attract admirers and made him contacts resulting in the publication of *Weary Blues,* his first book, and in a scholarship to attend Lincoln University in Pennsylvania, from which he was graduated in 1929.

Despite these strokes of fortune, Hughes, who was born in Missouri but lived in Harlem, New York for most of his adult life, did not have an easy existence. As a black, he suffered because of the slights given to the "darker brother," and most of his poems, novels, short stories, movie scripts, plays, songs, children's books, and biographies were concerned with the problems of blacks in America. His work reflects his sorrow, anger, or amusement at the plight of his characters, but is rarely bitter.

Hughes wrote in simple, rhythmic language that has been understood and appreciated by a great many people, both in this country and in the more than twenty-five countries where his work has appeared in translation. A man of deep feeling as well as intelligence, he wrote primarily for readers who respond with their hearts.

Mother to Son

Well, son, I'll tell you:
Life for me ain't been no crystal stair.
It's had tacks in it,
And splinters,
5   And boards torn up,
And places with no carpet on the floor—
Bare.

But all the time
I'se been a-climbin' on,
10   And reachin' landin's,
And turnin' corners,
And sometimes goin' in the dark
Where there ain't been no light.
So boy, don't you turn back.
15   Don't you set down on the steps
'Cause you finds it's kinder hard.
Don't you fall now—
For I'se still goin', honey,
I'se still climbin',
20   And life for me ain't been no crystal stair.

Meaning and Method

1. The poem is based on an extended metaphor (see the definition of metaphor in the Glossary) comparing the journey through life to a stairway one must climb. What words or phrases are used to extend the comparison? (For example, the tacks in the stairway show that it is not put together from the best materials and that one must be careful to avoid being injured. So the woman's life journey has been made more difficult by the shoddy treatment she has received and the shabby material objects which she can afford to support life. Such poverty and prejudice injure in a mental and spiritual sense.)
2. Do you think the comparison is appropriate? Explain how the journey through life is like climbing a stairway.
3. What images indicate that the journey through life has been difficult?
4. Does the speaker feel sorry for herself because she has had a hard life? What advice does she offer her son? What does her attitude show about her character?

Dream Deferred

What happens to a dream deferred?

    Does it dry up
    like a raisin in the sun?

    Or fester like a sore—
5   And then run?
    Does it stink like rotten meat?
    Or crust and sugar over—
    like a syrupy sweet?

    Maybe it just sags
10   like a heavy load.

    Or does it explode?

Meaning and Method

1. To defer means to postpone or to submit to another's wishes. Here Hughes compares the deferred dream to various physical things. In his similes, what happens to the dream because it is put off? Does it disappear? become less important? become transformed to something ugly and dangerous?
2. What verbs are used in the similes? What do they indicate about the advisability of deferring dreams?
3. What is the dream that has been deferred?
4. Why is the final line italicized?

Discussion and Composition

1. "Mother to Son" employs an extended metaphor. By adding details extend the metaphor in the last line of "Dream Deferred." Begin with "A dream deferred is _____." What thing that explodes will you identify the dream with?

2. In a short essay explain the meaning and appropriateness of each of the similes in "Dream Deferred."

MARGARET ABIGAIL WALKER
(born 1915)

"I Want to Write, I Want to Write the Songs of My People," the title of Miss Walker's first published poem, is in many respects the theme of her literary life. She was sixteen when the poem was published in *The Crisis,* the official magazine of the NAACP. Later she said, "As an adolescent, I wrote every single day I lived. It was like eating and sleeping and breathing, I guess. I wanted to express the feeling of the Negro people and my own especially."

Miss Walker, a minister's daughter, was born in Birmingham, Alabama. She lived in the South until she enrolled in Northwestern University. After her graduation, she moved to Chicago and worked at a variety of jobs—as a social worker, reporter, secretary, and magazine editor. In 1939, Miss Walker enrolled in the creative-writing program at the University of Iowa. Since graduating with a master's degree from Iowa, she has taught at various colleges in the South.

Her only book of poems, *For My People,* was published by Yale University as part of their Younger Poets Series. Miss Walker has also written a novel, *Jubilee* (1966), which she submitted as part of her work at the University of Iowa's Writers' Workshop. Her *Prophets for a New Day* was published in 1970 and *How I Wrote Jubilee* in 1972.

Iowa Farmer

I talked to a farmer one day in Iowa.
We looked out far over acres of wheat.
He spoke with pride and yet not boastfully;
he had no need to fumble for his words.
5   He knew his land and there was love for home
within the soft serene eyes of his son.
His ugly house was clean against the storm;
there was no hunger deep within the heart
nor burning riveted within the bone,
10   but here they ate a satisfying bread.
Yet in the Middle West where wheat was plentiful;
where grain grew golden under sunny skies
and cattle fattened through the summer heat
I could remember more familiar sights.

Meaning and Method

1. What words or phrases show that the Iowa wheat-farmer was a contented man? Did his son share his attitude? What do you think caused the farmer to feel contented?
2. Did the speaker share the feelings of the farmer? Why may lines 8 and 9 be interpreted literally and figuratively? What do you think are the "more familiar sights" the speaker remembers? How does the knowledge that the poet is black help you understand these lines?
3. Is the tone of the poem one of bitter envy? of sadness? of melancholy? something else?

THEODORE ROETHKE*
(1908–1963)

Roethke was born and grew up in Saginaw, Michigan, where his family owned an enormous greenhouse business (over twenty-five acres under glass). Playing and working in the greenhouses and outlying fields and forests gave him a great love for the beauty and integrity he saw in nature. The impact of these early experiences was to become evident in his poems, in which the land, wild creatures, plants, even greenhouses were to play such an important role. Symbols for life and creation provided by the surroundings of Roethke's boyhood surface again and again in his poems. Out of the green, ordered growing he remembered, Roethke created poems of both physical and spiritual struggle and growth.

By the time he reached college, Roethke felt drawn to poetry but did not receive any real encouragement until he was a graduate student at Harvard. From then on he wrote poetry with ever increasing skill and beauty, while he made a living teaching at various universities. Roethke's achievement was recognized and widely appreciated in his lifetime (he won every major literary award in the country, including a Pulitzer Prize and two National Book Awards), and his fame has continued to grow since his death.

Roethke's success as a poet was paralleled by his success as a teacher. He had the ability to communicate his immense energy and inspiration about literature to students, although it meant giving a great deal of himself. Colleagues have commented on the devotion and hard work his students gave Roethke in return.

Theodore Roethke's own words are perhaps the best advice for reading his superbly made poems: "approach these poems as a child would, naively, with your whole being awake, your faculties loose and alert. . . . *Listen* to them, for they are written to be heard."†

---

* **Roethke** (rath′kē).
† Quoted from Roethke's "Open Letter," *Mid-Century American Poets,* ed. John Ciardi (N.Y.: Twain Publishers, Inc., 1950), p. 68.

The Meadow Mouse

1

In a shoe box stuffed in an old nylon stocking
Sleeps the baby mouse I found in the meadow,
Where he trembled and shook beneath a stick
Till I caught him up by the tail and brought him in,
5   Cradled in my hand,
A little quaker, the whole body of him trembling,
His absurd whiskers sticking out like a cartoon-mouse,
His feet like small leaves,
Little lizard-feet,
10   Whitish and spread wide when he tried to struggle away,
Wriggling like a miniscule° puppy.

Now he's eaten his three kinds of cheese and drunk
    from his bottle-cap watering-trough—
So much he just lies in one corner,
His tail curled under him, his belly big
15   As his head; his bat-like ears
Twitching, tilting toward the least sound.

Do I imagine he no longer trembles
When I come close to him?
He seems no longer to tremble.

2

20   But this morning the shoe-box house on the back porch
    is empty.
Where has he gone, my meadow mouse,
My thumb of a child that nuzzled in my palm?—
To run under the hawk's wing,
Under the eye of the great owl watching from
    the elm tree,
25   To live by courtesy of the shrike,° the snake,
    the tom-cat.

11. miniscule: very small. **25. shrike:** a bird having a strong hooked beak; it often impales its insect prey on thorns.

I think of the nestling fallen into the deep grass,
The turtle gasping in the dusty rubble of the highway,
The paralytic stunned in the tub, and the water rising,—
All things innocent, hapless, forsaken.

Meaning and Method

1. Which images and similes in the first stanza of part 1 picture the fear of the mouse? What details of description in stanza two contrast those of the first? What image reveals that the creature is still wary?
2. What is the speaker's attitude toward the mouse? Why does he take the mouse in?
3. When the speaker discovers the mouse gone "to run under the hawk's wing," what do we understand about the mouse's instincts?
4. Does this understanding change the attitude of the speaker? What does the mouse's leaving make him feel sorry for?

Discussion and Composition

1. Have you ever adopted a wild creature, perhaps because it was injured and helpless, or because its parents had been killed? What would you do if you found one in a situation like this? What do you feel might be the outcome of the relationship?

2. In a paper of one or two paragraphs, explain why you would or would not adopt the creature and, if you did adopt it, how you would feel about keeping it as a pet or returning it to the wilds.

DENNIS SCHMITZ
(born 1937)

Dennis Schmitz was born in a small Iowa town on the Mississippi River. He attended local Catholic schools: a military high school and Loras College, from which he received a B.A. in 1959. He attended graduate school at the University of Chicago while at the same time making a living teaching at nearby schools. After receiving his M.A. in 1961, he taught at the University of Wisconsin in Milwaukee. Since 1966 he has taught writing, English, and foreign literature in translation at California State University in Sacramento.

Schmitz still enjoys wandering and fishing the delta areas near his present home, just as he wandered and fished the Mississippi where he grew up. This solitude and contact with natural things remain important to Schmitz's vision, as his poetry shows. Out of the long looks and daydreaming these excursions allow come the raw materials for many of his poems. They have a terse, honest cleanness, and their observations of death and birth in nature and of human rituals are pared by a tough, insightful objectivity.

The poems Schmitz has published fill fewer and slimmer volumes than those of many of his contemporaries, but their quality and strength more than make up for their smaller number. His first book, *We Weep for Our Strangeness,* was four years in the making, but its quality won for it the Big Table Series of Younger Poets Award in 1969. The shape of his poems on the page and the line breaks help create a sense of movement important in his work. These techniques are amply illustrated in the following selection, "The Wounded Doe."

The Wounded Doe

steps out of the green
& yellow handsful
of leaves still on the trees
her soft ears

5   tremble like butterflies

berries are crushed
against her coat
    &
her wet breath crumbles
10   white
on her muzzle

all the bones of her body
are braced
against her teeth

15   & I am so close

I can hear the slow

fingers of blood working
away from her skull
as her death
20   drains into her body

& she waits to fall

Meaning and Method

1. The speaker is very close to the doe. What details in the poem give us that same feeling of being very close? Do you think the close-up view makes the poem's observations more effective? Explain why or why not.
2. The poem contrasts the life of the doe with her death. The poet's choice of verbs helps to build this contrast. Point out which verbs give you a sense of living tenseness and which a sense of giving way to death.
3. Why do you think the poet has used so many images which observe the living functions of the doe? How do the descriptions of breathing, muscle tenseness, and circulating blood emphasize the coming of death? (For example, breath shows life, but her breath is crumbling, and crumbling is associated with giving way. The giving way of something living means death.)

Compare and Contrast

Both "The Meadow Mouse" and "The Wounded Doe" say something about the wild animal's struggle to survive and the inevitability of its death. In each poem, what is the attitude of the speaker toward the creature?

MAY SWENSON
(born 1919)

May Swenson was born in Logan, Utah and was educated at Utah State University. She worked as a reporter on Salt Lake City's *Desert News* before moving to New York, where she has been an editor with several publishing houses. Her poems have appeared in such magazines as *Poetry, The Nation, The New Yorker* and *Harper's.* She has won many awards and honors, including the National Institute of Arts and Letters Award in 1960 and the Shelley Poetry Award in 1968. Her books of poetry include *Another Animal, To Mix With Time, Poems to Solve,* and *Half Sun Half Sleep.*

May Swenson writes herself that the experience of poetry is "based on a craving to get through the curtain of things as they *appear,* to things as they *are,* and then into the larger, wider space of things as they are becoming."

Her fellow poet, Elizabeth Bishop, has said of her art: "Miss Swenson looks and sees, and rejoices in what she sees. Her poems are varied, energetic and full of a directness and optimism that are unusual in these days of formulated despair and/or careful stylishness."

Question

Body my house
my horse my hound
what will I do
when you are fallen

5   Where will I sleep
How will I ride
What will I hunt

Where can I go
without my mount
10   all eager and quick
How will I know
in thicket ahead
is danger or treasure
when Body my good
15   bright dog is dead

How will it be
to lie in the sky
without roof or door
and wind for an eye

20   With cloud for shift°
how will I hide?

20. shift: a loose dress.

Meaning and Method

1. What three things are the speaker's body identified with? These
   may at first seem unlikely. What aspect of the body does each of
   the metaphors emphasize? How are these images appropriate?
2. The language of this poem is deceptively simple; the subject
   seems to be about abstract qualities. What descriptions of actions
   make the poem vivid and concrete?

PERSONIFICATION AND APOSTROPHE

Poets find a useful tool in another figure of speech, *personification*. When an object, animal, or idea is *personified*, it is given human qualities. This device is not intended to persuade us that the thing (or animal or idea) personified is literally human but to make us experience it more personally, in relation to human feelings which we understand. When well made, a personification can strike a chord of recognition and harmony in us for the things of our world. Personification domesticates, makes more human, things that are alien to us. For instance, Emily Dickinson personifies the wind (p. 41) as "A rapid, footless guest" whose fingers "let go a music." This embodiment rings true; the sounds and movements caused by the wind can be compared to human sounds and movements, and the imaginative effect of the personification vitalizes the whole poem. In Louise Bogan's poem "Musician" (p. 45), the instrument "Sings as it wished to sing," having been given a capacity for expression of emotion that helps us see how much life the musician gives the instrument.

Apostrophe allows the poet to speak directly to an object or animal as if it were capable of human understanding (or to an absent person as if he or she were capable of hearing and replying). For example, in "Beat! Beat! Drums!" Walt Whitman directs orders to the drums and bugles as if they could hear and obey. (See the Glossary definition for examples of apostrophe used with personification.)

EMILY DICKINSON
(1830–1886)

Although biographers know many facts about Emily Dickinson, they understand very little about her. They know that she led an outwardly simple life—that she never married, and, except for two trips with her father, spent all her life in Amherst, Massachusetts. They know that she studied for a year at Mount Holyoke Seminary (now College), a few miles from her home. Despite many guesses, however, no biographer understands exactly why she began to withdraw from the world in her early twenties or why she eventually became a recluse.

In her self-imposed isolation she communicated with friends by writing letters in which she sometimes enclosed poems. But no one dreamed that she had written nearly 1800 poems and fragments, found only after her death. Some of these were on sheets of paper tied neatly together. Others were on scraps of paper, such as the backs of invitations or brown paper bags.

The richness of the poems themselves was even more amazing than their existence. Startlingly precise, imaginative metaphors reflected Emily Dickinson's unique way of looking at the world. Emily Dickinson chose words whose connotations and sound qualities compress a large or complex idea into a small space. As a result, her poems, like her life, often seem simple on the surface but are sometimes difficult to understand.

The Wind Tapped Like a Tired Man

The Wind—tapped like a tired Man—
And like a Host—"Come in"
I boldly answered—entered then
My Residence within

5   A Rapid—footless Guest—
To offer whom a Chair
Were as impossible as hand
A Sofa to the Air—

No Bone had He to bind Him—
10 His Speech was like the Push
Of numerous Humming Birds at once
From a superior Bush—

His Countenance—a Billow—
His Fingers, as He passed
15 Let go a music—as of tunes
Blown tremulous° in Glass—

He visited—still flitting—
Then like a timid Man
Again, He tapped—'twas flurriedly°—
20 And I became alone—

16. tremulous (trem′yǝ·lǝs): trembling.   **19. flurriedly:** excitedly or nervously.

Meaning and Method

1. Does the fact that the speaker personifies the wind—and specifically sees it as a guest—indicate that she is isolated? lonely? sensitive? something else? What other details in the poem help characterize her?
2. What words or phrases make you see or feel the movement of the wind? What sounds in lines 10–12 give you the impression of the sound of the wind? In your answer, tell why the effect of lines 10–12 would change if you substituted *many* for *numerous* (line 11).
3. Describe in your own words the character of the wind. Support your description by reference to specific details in the poem. Do you think the speaker's change from thinking of the wind as a "tired man" (line 1) to a "timid man" (line 18) indicates that she is disappointed with it? Why or why not?

Composition

Rewrite this poem, opening with the following line: "The wind knocked like an angry man." Make other changes in the poem accordingly. Note how the first verb gives focus to the entire poem.

WALTER DE LA MARE
(1873–1956)

Things just outside the limits of reality—dreams, magic, ghosts—fascinated de la Mare. Surprisingly, he held onto his belief in the mystery and beauty of life despite eighteen years of working at a humdrum job in a London oil company.

His distinctive talent, evident in many poems published during this time, eventually freed him from his job. At the age of thirty-six, he was granted a British government pension to enable him to write full time. The results of this freedom to write are more than fifty volumes of poetry, fiction, and essays, most of which are marked by his special brand of fantasy.

Silver

Slowly, silently, now the moon
Walks the night in her silver shoon;°
This way, and that, she peers, and sees
Silver fruit upon silver trees;
5 One by one the casements° catch
Her beams beneath the silvery thatch;°
Couched in his kennel, like a log,
With paws of silver sleeps the dog;
From their shadowy cote° the white breasts peep
10 Of doves in a silver-feathered sleep;
A harvest mouse goes scampering by,
With silver claws and a silver eye;
And moveless fish in the water gleam,
By silver reeds in a silver stream.

2. shoon: shoes.   **5. casements:** windows.   **6. thatch:** straw used for roofs.   **9. cote** (kōt): a shed or coop.

Meaning and Method

1. Why, in your opinion, does the poet personify the moon? Why does he not say instead that the moon shines?

2. Notice the frequent use of /s/, /sh/, and /l/ sounds. How do they help to create an atmosphere of peacefulness? Read the poem aloud before you answer.

3. Why do you think de la Mare called his poem "Silver" rather than "Moonlight"? In your answer, discuss the connotations of each word.

Composition

1. Write a descriptive paragraph about an object which you consider beautiful or ugly. By means of specific details which appeal to the senses of sight and touch, try to make the reader see and feel the beauty or ugliness of the object or scene you describe.

2. Write a composition in which you imagine the wind and moon meeting. Show the characteristics of each through their words and actions.

Compare and Contrast

Both "The Wind Tapped Like a Tired Man" and "Silver" personify a natural thing. What human qualities have been given to the wind? to the moon? Do the personalities associated with each seem appropriate?

LOUISE BOGAN
(1897–1970)

A woman who wrote, encouraged, and appraised poetry and remained a major force in American letters for half a century, Louise Bogan valued a life of privacy and anonymity most highly. She was born and educated in New England and lived in that area for most of her life, although she traveled abroad on occasion. Both her marriages were marked by tragedy. In 1920, after only four years of marriage, her first husband died, leaving her alone with a daughter. Her marriage in 1925 to poet Raymond Holden ended in divorce twelve years later. At various times, Bogan suffered breakdowns, but each time she recovered and continued her work as poet, critic, and journalist. Although she kept private the struggles that marked her personal world, she earned a highly esteemed position in the literary world.

While she maintained the seclusion that she valued, Bogan wielded a quiet power that made her a shaping force for other poets (for example, young Theodore Roethke (see p. 32) sought her advice and criticism) as well as an admired lyric poet. From the first, she received acclaim for her writing. Prizes and honors accrued steadily over the years. A special mark of her greatness is the high admiration she received from fellow writers for both her artfully crafted poems and her unerringly truthful but witty and graceful criticism.

Her poems contain powerful emotions within an equally powerful, controlled style, giving Louise Bogan's work what has been described as "a passionate austerity, a subtle balance." *

* Quoted from *Modern American Literature,* Vol. IV, supplement to the fourth edition, ed. Dorothy Nyren, et al. (N.Y.: Frederick Ungar, 1976).

Musician

Where have these hands been,
By what delayed,
That so long stayed
Apart from the thin

5   Strings which they now grace
          With their lonely skill?
          Music and their cool will
          At last interlace.

          Now with great ease, and slow,
10   The thumb, the finger, the strong
          Delicate hand plucks the long
          String it was born to know.

          And, under the palm, the string
          Sings as it wished to sing.

Meaning and Method

1. What details show the musician's mastery of the instrument? Why might the hands' skill be described as "cool" (line 7) and "lonely" (line 6)?
2. Who or what receives satisfaction and a sense of completeness from the joining of talented hands and instrument? the musician? the speaker? the instrument? What line tells you that the instrument has been given human feelings?

Composition

Write a poem or essay in which you describe how the skill of an expert, such as an Olympic skier or a great sculptor, makes you feel about the sport, trade, or art that has been mastered. Be sure to include description of the way in which the master moves or handles the instruments of his or her profession.

CHRISTOPHER MORLEY
(1890–1957)

For Christopher Morley, the words of the English language were like a variety of tools, fascinating for their own sake and for the many things that could be made with them. Morley used these tools to write more than fifty volumes of essays, short stories, novels, plays, and poems. In one of his books, *The Trojan Horse,* he even combined verse, prose, and drama.

Morley, who was born in Haverford, Pennsylvania, graduated from Haverford College and went on to become a Rhodes Scholar at Oxford University. From the time his first book was published, when he was twenty-two, he won critical praise for his wit and skill with words. However, although his style remained witty, as he grew older he became increasingly concerned with the serious problems of living in the modern world. Particularly in the last three decades of his life, the bright surface of his work covered a deep pessimism in his outlook on the future.

Nursery Rhyme
for the Tender-Hearted

Scuttle, scuttle, little roach—
How you run when I approach:
Up above the pantry shelf,
Hastening to secrete yourself.

5   Most adventurous of vermin,
How I wish I could determine
How you spend your hours of ease,
Perhaps reclining on the cheese.

Cook has gone, and all is dark—
10   Then the kitchen is your park:
In the garbage heap that she leaves
Do you browse among the tea leaves?

How delightful to suspect
All the places you have trekked:
15 Does your long antenna whisk its
Gentle tip across the biscuits?

Do you linger, little soul,
Drowsing in our sugar bowl?
Or, abandonment most utter,
20 Shake a shimmy° on the butter?

Do you chant your simple tunes
Swimming in the baby's prunes?
Then, when dawn comes, do you slink
Homeward to the kitchen sink?

25 Timid roach, why be so shy?
We are brothers, thou and I.
In the midnight, like yourself,
I explore the pantry shelf!

20. **shimmy:** a dance in which you shake your hips.

Meaning and Method

1. What do you think of when you hear the word *roach?* What is unusual about the speaker's approach to the insect?
2. Considering most people's reaction to roaches, explain why you think that the speaker did *not* mean the following: "How *delightful* to suspect/All the places you have trekked." Why is the word *trekked* appropriate to describe the roach's activities? What connotations does this word have that the word *walked,* for example, does not have?
3. Do you think that the speaker is one of the tender-hearted to whom he dedicated this poem? Why or why not? After reading the poem, explain why you think the title is not ironic.*
4. The poet uses apostrophe when he addresses the "little roach" in line 1. Where else does he use it? Does his use of apostrophe ever seem ironic? Why or why not?

* Irony exists when a writer says something in such a way that the opposite meaning is implied.

Composition

The war between the Greeks and the Trojans, described in Homer's *Iliad,* was won because of the Greeks' use of the Trojan horse. Look up the story of the Trojan horse in a dictonary or book of mythology, and then write a stanza or two which you start with the line: "Welcome, welcome, Trojan horse." Or write a poem starting with: "Welcome, welcome, hurricane," "Welcome, welcome, midterm test."

CARL SANDBURG
(1878–1967)

The son of poor Swedish immigrants who had settled in Galesburg, Illinois, Sandburg had to leave school at thirteen to earn money by doing various menial jobs. After serving in the Spanish-American War, he worked as a fireman to put himself through college but left after four years of study—without a degree—to become a journalist. Eventually, he became a successful reporter and columnist for a major Chicago newspaper.

Sandburg's talents as a writer, however, were not confined to journalistic prose. He won Pulitzer Prizes for both biography and poetry and had a wider audience than most poets have because he wrote poems that workers, farmers, and shopkeepers could understand. He wrote, as he said, the "poetry of ordinary things," such as fences, telephone wires, city life, the feeling of being lost. He "put America on paper," in the words of one commentator, and he put American speech on paper, too, by using colloquial expressions and slang in his poems. In addition, he wrote in free verse which is close to the rhythms of everyday American speech.

Much of Sandburg's life and work can be summed up in the phrase, *The People, Yes,* which he used as the title for one of his many books of poems. Sandburg believed that the people had created unrecognized poetry, and so he traveled around the country singing their folk songs, accompanying himself on a guitar or a banjo. Instead of isolating himself, he saw and understood the problems and rewards of "ordinary" people in both city and country. And he came up with a judgment about them that might be applied to some of his own poems: "The people will live on."

Jazz Fantasia

Drum on your drums, batter on your banjos, sob on the long cool winding saxophones. Go to it, O jazzmen.

Sling your knuckles on the bottoms of the happy tin pans, let your trombones ooze, and go husha-husha-hush with the slippery sandpaper.

Moan like an autumn wind high in the lonesome treetops, moan soft like you wanted somebody terrible, cry like a racing car slipping away from a motorcycle cop, bang-bang! you jazzmen, bang altogether drums, traps,° banjos, horns, tin cans—make two people fight on the top of a stairway and scratch each other's eyes in a clinch tumbling down the stairs.

Can the rough stuff. . . . Now a Mississippi steamboat pushes up the night river with a hoo-hoo-hoo-oo . . . and the green lanterns calling to the high soft stars. . . . a red moon rides on the humps of the low river hills. . . . Go to it, O jazzmen.

3. traps: percussion instruments, such as drums and cymbals, which are sounded by striking.

Meaning and Method

1. In the first two stanzas, Sandburg not only gives his impression of the sounds made by various instruments in a Dixieland jazz band, but in some cases indicates the way they look as well. What types of sound, and what sights, are indicated by the phrases "sob on the long cool winding saxophones" and "let your trombones ooze"?
2. In the third and fourth stanzas, the poet indicates the various stages through which the music passes. For example, the phrase *bang-bang!* indicates that the music at that point is fast and loud. At what other points is it fast and loud? When is it slow and soft? sad? gay?
3. The speaker talks to the jazzmen throughout the poem. Does his manner of talking to them make him seem involved in, or detached from, the music they create? Why?

Composition

Sandburg associated certain emotions or sensations with a specific type of music and the instruments used to create it. For example, the tin pans seemed "happy" to him, and the saxophone "cool" and sad. The music also called up visual images for him, such as "a red moon rides on the humps of the low river hills."

Listen to some instrumental music—jazz, classical, or modern—and write down the emotions, colors, images, or scenes which the music brings to mind. (The images do not have to be based on reality. A piece of music may make you think of blue camels or of a green sky.) Then attempt to organize these emotions and images into a stanza or two of free verse.

Compare and Contrast

Both "Musician" and "Jazz Fantasia" value music and musicians. What do you think are the main differences in the kinds of music each poem concerns? How do you imagine the jazz instrumentalists and the artist of "Musician" differ in the way they perform? How do the carefully formed, rhyming stanzas of one poem suit its type of music? How do the less formal, more rambling stanzas of the other suit its type?

WALT WHITMAN
(1819–1892)

In "Song of Myself," one of the poems that changed the course of American poetry, Whitman identified himself as "Walt Whitman, an American, one of the roughs."

This "rough," the son of a carpenter, was born in New York on Long Island, and grew up in Brooklyn. After only five years of formal schooling, he was apprenticed to a printer. In his twenties, he successively became a printer, a political reporter, and a newspaper editor who passionately editorialized against slavery.

Whitman at this time occasionally wrote verse in conventional meters and on conventional themes. But in 1848, after a trip which allowed him to see much of the variety, richness, and expanse of America, he began to write spirited free verse poems celebrating America and his own life. When the first edition of his book of poems, *Leaves of Grass* (for which he set the type), was published in 1855, it was clear that a new voice had arrived in American poetry.

Although most of Whitman's contemporaries disapproved of the work, *Leaves of Grass* pioneered vital changes in American poetry in both style and subject matter—changes which were to be appreciated fully only after his death. First, Whitman showed that free verse, which had been used infrequently before his time, was uniquely suited to the natural rhythms of American speech. Second, instead of imitating English literary subjects, Whitman wrote about his country and himself. In addition, he introduced strong emotional tones into American poetry. Whitman's poems are filled with joyful appreciation of the wonders of the world, and sorrow and horror at the ravages of war.

Beat! Beat! Drums!

Beat! beat! drums!—blow! bugles! blow!
Through the windows—through doors—burst like
 a ruthless force,
Into the solemn church, and scatter the congregation,
Into the school where the scholar is studying;

5   Leave not the bridegroom quiet—no happiness must he
         have now with his bride,
     Nor the peaceful farmer any peace, ploughing his field
         or gathering his grain,
     So fierce you whirr and pound you drums—so shrill
         you bugles blow.

     Beat! beat! drums!—blow! bugles! blow!
     Over the traffic of cities—over the rumble of wheels
         in the streets;
10   Are beds prepared for sleepers at night in the houses?
         no sleepers must sleep in those beds,
     No bargainers' bargains by day—no brokers or speculators
         —would they continue?
     Would the talkers be talking? would the singer attempt
         to sing?
     Would the lawyer rise in the court to state his case
         before the judge?
     Then rattle quicker, heavier drums—you bugles
         wilder blow.

15   Beat! beat! drums!—blow! bugles! blow!
     Make no parley—stop for no expostulation,°
     Mind not the timid—mind not the weeper or prayer,
     Mind not the old man beseeching the young man,
     Let not the child's voice be heard, nor the mother's
         entreaties,
20   Make even the trestles° to shake the dead where they lie
         awaiting the hearses,
     So strong you thump O terrible drums—so loud
         you bugles blow.

16. expostulation: earnest argument, usually for protest.   **20. trestles:** beams or bars supported by four legs, for bearing a platform.

Meaning and Method

1. What words or sounds in the first stanza help convey an impression of the disruption the bugles and drums—that is, war—will cause? How does the punctuation add to this impression of disruption?

2. What words describing the bugles and drums convey an impression of their harshness or disharmony? Which words are onomatopoeic?*
3. Apostrophe is used in this poem to create the impression that the speaker is giving orders to the bugles and drums. Give several examples of this technique, and explain whether the harsh effect of the poem would have been the same if, for example, *Make no parley* had been changed to *You should not make a parley*.
4. Does the speaker really want the bugles and drums to do what he is telling them to do? Does he feel resentment? anger? sorrow? horror? exultation for the war? Consider the tempo or pace of the poem before you answer. (For example, a sorrowful poem would probably be read slowly, a happy poem rapidly.)

Composition

Whitman's approach to human life is shown in his statement, "For my enemy is dead, a man divine as myself is dead." Explain what Whitman means by this statement. Then tell why you think one's attitude toward the enemy should be like or unlike Whitman's. Give a specific example of an "enemy"—real or imaginary—to support your points.

* Onomatopoeic (on'ə·mot'ə·pē'ĭk) words imitate the natural sounds they represent.

SYMBOL

In general, a *symbol* is an object which stands for something else in our mind's eye. The object is itself, of course, but it also means something further to us. When we think of a lion, we first identify the animal itself, but we also associate the lion with courage; we would say the lion is a symbol of courage. A cross is first of all an object with a certain form, but it also symbolizes certain aspects of Christianity.

In poetry, too, a symbol is something which means what it is and something more. Because of its symbolic quality, an object becomes tied to some other idea or emotion or abstract quality. In "Do Not Go Gentle Into That Good Night," Dylan Thomas speaks to his dying father,

> Do not go gentle into that good night.
> Rage, rage against the dying of the light.

Night means the period of darkness in a day, a time when we sleep. But it also is often used (as it is here) as a symbol for death, with the loss of light representing the loss of life.

A number of symbols poets may use are easily recognizable. Night or winter generally symbolize death; the red rose stands for passionate love; a road or path, for the journey through life. However, a reader cannot take the meaning of a symbol for granted. Sometimes a poet will create a special meaning for an object. Only by the context of the whole poem do we know that it has the weight of a symbol.

For example, in Robert Frost's "The Tuft of Flowers" (p. 61) the speaker has discovered a field which a man had mowed earlier that morning and then left. A butterfly leads him to a clump of flowers which the mower left standing. On a literal level, the flowers provide relief for the eye and a haven for the butterfly. But the speaker feels uplifted by this unselfish salute to the beauty and vitality of nature; in these spared flowers, the speaker finds a common bond with the mower, and the tuft of flowers becomes a symbol for a spiritual and human use of nature.

The symbol plays an important part in the poems in which it is well used. It is a concrete thing we can perceive with the senses; it has a place in the poem as the object itself. In the course of the poem, however, the reader also comes to see it as representing something else. Hence the symbol gives the poem more weight, more levels of meaning.

ARNA BONTEMPS*
(1902–1973)

For many years Bontemps lived alternately in the North and the South. He was born in Louisiana in 1902, went to college in California, and taught in Harlem, Alabama, and Chicago. He finally settled in Nashville, Tennessee, where he held the post of chief librarian at Fisk University from 1943 to 1965, resigning only to work in the university's public relations office.

From his early twenties on, Bontemps wrote steadily in his spare time, producing poems, short stories, novels, children's books, and biographies. Like Langston Hughes, with whom he collaborated on collections of black poetry and folklore, his work is primarily about the black people. His first novel is about a black jockey. (The musical *St. Louis Woman* was later based on it.) His second and third novels are about slave revolts. In all of his work, he emphasizes the black people's sense of worth and dignity.

* **Bontemps:** The name is of French origin. Because Bontemps was born in Louisiana, the name is pronounced *bawn′tămp,* in the Louisiana French dialect. In Parisian French, it would be pronounced *bōn′tawn.*

The Day-Breakers

We are not come to wage a strife
   With swords upon this hill.
It is not wise to waste the life
   Against a stubborn will.
5   Yet would we die as some have done,
Beating a way for the rising sun.

Meaning and Method

1. What kind of strife does the speaker wish to avoid? What kind of struggle does he think worth dying for? In your answer, explain what you think the speaker means by "Beating a way for the rising sun."
2. In the context of this poem, what might the rising sun symbolize?

Composition

Write a composition contrasting the attitudes of the speakers in "The Day-Breakers" and "Mother to Son" or "Dream Deferred." Which speaker would be more active in the struggle for civil rights? Why? Which poem do you think would have more effect on the outcome of the struggle? Why?

ROBERT FROST
(1874–1963)

For Robert Frost, the road to recognition and fame was as rocky as the soil of New England which he had tried to farm. His father died when Frost was eleven, and the boy came with his mother from San Francisco, his birthplace, to the East Coast. After graduating as valedictorian of his high school class in Lawrence, Massachusetts, he set out on a stubbornly independent path which for many years led to worldly failure.

He attended Dartmouth and Harvard colleges but never earned a degree. As a husband and father, he barely managed to support his family by farming and teaching in New Hampshire. Most of his poems were rejected by the editors of the American magazines and publishing houses to which he sent them.

Searching for a more responsive environment, he and his family moved in 1912 to a farm in England. In the next two years he published two books there, winning enthusiastic critical acclaim and praise for being "so American" a poet and bringing the rural life and speech of New England into poetry. In 1915 Frost returned to an admiring American public eager to read the poet's work.

For nearly half a century afterward, he continued to write original and significant poems, while honors—including four Pulitzer Prizes for poetry and numerous honorary university degrees—were heaped upon him. Perhaps the greatest tribute to him occurred in 1961, when he became the first poet in American history to speak at the inauguration of a President, that of John F. Kennedy.

By the time of his death, Frost was in many ways the national poet of America. Millions of Americans admired his outspoken personality and responded to the rural characters in his poems, who talked in everyday language and rhythms. But Frost's poems are rarely as simple as they seem, for they are full of subtle ironies, connotative images, and words with many levels of meaning. In his complexity, Frost was true to his subject: he wrote about reality, and reality—rural or urban—is not simple.

The Tuft of Flowers

I went to turn the grass once after one
Who mowed it in the dew before the sun.

The dew was gone that made his blade so keen
Before I came to view the leveled scene.

5   I looked for him behind an isle of trees;
I listened for his whetstone° on the breeze.

But he had gone his way, the grass all mown,
And I must be, as he had been—alone,

"As all must be," I said within my heart,
10   "Whether they work together or apart."

But as I said it, swift there passed me by
On noiseless wing a bewildered butterfly,

Seeking with memories grown dim o'er night
Some resting flower of yesterday's delight.

15   And once I marked° his flight go round and round,
As where some flower lay withering on the ground.

And then he flew as far as eye could see,
And then on tremulous wing came back to me.

I thought of questions that have no reply,
20   And would have turned to toss the grass to dry;

But he turned first, and led my eye to look
At a tall tuft of flowers beside a brook,

A leaping tongue of bloom the scythe had spared
Beside a reedy brook the scythe had bared.

6. **whetstone:** a stone to sharpen metal instruments or tools.
15. **marked:** noticed.

25   The mower in the dew had loved them thus,
       By leaving them to flourish, not for us,

       Nor yet to draw one thought of ours to him,
       But from sheer morning gladness at the brim.

       The butterfly and I had lit upon,
30   Nevertheless, a message from the dawn,

       That made me hear the wakening birds around,
       And hear his long scythe whispering to the ground,

       And feel a spirit kindred to my own;
       So that henceforth I worked no more alone;

35   But glad with him, I worked as with his aid,
       And weary, sought at noon with him the shade;

       And dreaming, as it were, held brotherly speech
       With one whose thought I had not hoped to reach.

       "Men work together," I told him from the heart,
40   "Whether they work together or apart."

Meaning and Method

1. In order for hay to be made, the tall grass must first be mowed down and then turned over to dry in the sun. Is the speaker's mood when he comes to turn the grass one of enthusiasm? desolation? something else? In your answer, comment on the connotations of *leveled* (line 4), and on lines 8–10.
2. Why is the butterfly "bewildered" (line 12)? Why does he fly around a "withering" flower (line 16)?
3. Why did the mower leave the tuft of flowers? What change occurs in the speaker's mood when he sees it? Why does he no longer feel alone?
4. Explain the meaning of the last two lines. What idea do they express about bonds between people and their relationship to nature? Why does finding the tuft of flowers cause the speaker to change his mind about working together?

EDNA ST. VINCENT MILLAY
(1892–1950)

A passionate desire for new experiences characterized Edna St. Vincent Millay as a young girl growing up in Maine, as a student at Vassar College, and as a writer and actress in Greenwich Village. She was proud of her intense approach to life, and defiant about the dangers, as the following poem from her Village days shows:

> My candle burns at both ends;
> It will not last the night;
> But ah, my foes, and oh, my friends—
> It gives a lovely light!

The "candle" of Millay's poetic talents did burn fast and bright. At nineteen, she wrote "Renascence," the long poem with which she first won fame; by the time she was thirty-one, she had won a Pulitzer Prize for poetry. Her personal lyrics expressed the feelings of a generation of romantic young rebels, bringing her tremendous popularity.

Shortly after the age of thirty, however, both her life and her poetry underwent a striking change. In 1923, she married Eugen Boissevain and moved to the farm in Austerlitz, New York, which was to be her home until her death. Increasingly, her poems became more somber, less devoted to explorations of her own feelings and more to social problems.

Although some critics prefer the romantic lyrics, others see a deeper talent in the later poems. Most critics, however, feel that in her best lyrics, old and new, she exhibits both rare talent and rare accomplishment.

This Door You Might Not Open, and You Did

This door you might not open, and you did;
So enter now, and see for what slight thing
You are betrayed. . . . Here is no treasure hid,

No cauldron,° no clear crystal mirroring
5   The sought-for truth, no heads of women slain
For greed like yours, no writhings of distress,
But only what you see. . . . Look yet again—
An empty room, cobwebbed and comfortless.

Yet this alone out of my life I kept
10   Unto myself, lest any know me quite;
And you did so profane° me when you crept
Unto the threshold of this room to-night
That I must never more behold your face.
This now is yours. I seek another place.

privacy violated

4. cauldron: large kettle or boiler, often associated with witches.
11. profane: show lack of respect or reverence for.

Meaning and Method

1. The room in "This Door You Might Not Open, and You Did" stands for something other than itself, something that is not directly mentioned in the poem. What quality or aspect of the speaker might the room represent?
2. Why is the speaker angry with the person addressed? Why does the speaker want the room kept private? Why must the speaker never behold the other's face?
3. This poem suggests other hidden rooms in literature: the room where Bluebeard kept his murdered wives and the cave where Ali Baba discovered the treasure of the forty thieves. How is this room different? What does it actually contain? Is it used often or infrequently?

Compare and Contrast

What two opposite needs of human beings are shown in the poem "The Tuft of Flowers" and this sonnet by Millay? Does one poem contradict the other? That is, does accepting the ideas of one force a rejection of the ideas of the other? Explain.

ELINOR WYLIE
(1885–1928)

The literary career of Elinor [Hoyt] Wylie was limited almost entirely to the last seven years of her life. As a young girl growing up in Philadelphia and Washington society, she had considered writing as a profession. But it was not until after she was divorced from her second husband, Horace Wylie, that she began to write extensively. Her third husband, William Rose Benét, a poet himself, introduced her to the literary life of New York City and encouraged her to write.

Her collection of poems, *Nets to Catch the Wind* (1921), impressed critics, who praised her technical brilliance and her ability to capture subtle moods. Her subsequent volumes—*Black Armour* (1923), *Trivial Breath* (1928), *Angels and Earthly Creatures* (1929)—won even higher praise. Mrs. Wylie also wrote four novels—*Jennifer Lorn* (1923), *The Venetian Glass Nephew* (1925), *The Orphan Angel* (1926), and *Mr. Hodge and Mr. Hazard* (1928).

According to the poet Louise Bogan, Mrs. Wylie's poetry is marked by her "ability to fuse thought and passion into the most admirable and complex forms." Moreover, she displays the "craftman's concern for phrasing and for the particular qualities of words." Her vivid images and her use of sound patterns to convey moods and feelings make her poems exciting yet delicate.

Sanctuary

This is the bricklayer; hear the thud
Of his heavy load dumped down on stone.
His lustrous bricks are brighter than blood,
His smoking mortar whiter than bone.

5   Set each sharp-edged, fire-bitten brick
Straight by the plumb-line's shivering length;
Make my marvelous wall so thick
Dead nor living may shake its strength.

Full as a crystal cup with drink
10   Is my cell with dreams, and quiet, and cool.
Stop, old man! You must leave a chink;
How can I breathe? *You can't, you fool!*

Meaning and Method

1. How does the speaker's attitude towards the bricklayer change
in this poem?
2. At what point do you realize that something sinister is going on
in this poem? How is the suspense maintained?

Compare and Contrast

How does the sanctuary in this poem resemble the room in
Edna St. Vincent Millay's poem (explain lines 9 and 10)? How
does it differ?

Composition

This short poem contains the germ of a suspense or murder
story. Invent a short narrative explaining why the bricklayer
might want to wall in the speaker of the poem.

DAVID P. YOUNG
(born 1936)

David Young was raised and educated in the Midwest. Born in Davenport, Iowa, he also lived in Nebraska and Minnesota. After receiving his undergraduate degree from Carleton College in Minnesota, he attended Yale University in Connecticut, from which he received his Ph.D. in 1964. Meanwhile, he had begun teaching at Oberlin College in Ohio, where he still teaches and also edits the literary magazine, *Field: Contemporary Poetry and Poetics*.

At the same time, Young has pursued his writing career with success. His first book, *Sweating Out the Winter,* won the 1968 U.S. Award from the International Poetry Forum. Besides continuing his poetry, he has translated poems of Italian, German, and Chinese poets, written literary criticism, and actively involved himself in the world of printing (he owns part interest in a press in Oberlin).

The effect of the Midwest is apparent in his poems, in which Young says he strives for a "spare American music." The following selection, "The Man Who Swallowed a Bird," illustrates two elements of his style: a mixture of tones and the use of complex, sometimes surreal, images*. It also treats two themes which concern Young: imagination and metamorphosis. What emerges most frequently from his poetry is a voice quietly reaching "for something just outside the room he lives in,"† blending past and present, the ideal and the real.

---

* Surreal images create dreamlike or fantastic effects by unexpected or incongruous combinations and juxtapositions. Though their appearance and arrangement seem to arise from chance, they are the result of a conscious effort to reproduce such images of the unconscious as are seen in dreams.
† Quoted from *Contemporary Poets,* ed. James Vinson (London: St. James Press, 1975).

The Man Who Swallowed a Bird

Happened when he was yawning.
A black or scarlet bird went down his throat

And disappeared, and at the time
He only looked foolish, belched a feather;
5 The change took time.

But when we saw him again in the
Half-dusk of a summer evening
He was a different man. His eyes
Glittered and his brown hands
10 Lived in the air like swallows;
Knowledge of season lit his face
But he seemed restless. What he said
Almost made sense, but from a distance:

 Once I swallowed a bird,
15 Felt like a cage at first, but now
 Sometimes my flesh flutters and I think
 I could go mad for joy.

In the fall he vanished. South
Some said, others said dead. Jokes
20 About metamorphosis° were made. Nonetheless,
Some of us hear odd songs.
       Suppose
You press your ear against the morning air,
Above and on your left you might
25 Hear music that implies without a word
A world where a man can absorb a bird.

20. metamorphosis (mĕt′ə-môr′fə-sĭs): a change in structure, form or character.

Meaning and Method

1. A bird lives close to the earth but is able to soar above it. In this poem it symbolizes a spirit of freedom linked with nature. Reread the last stanza, then explain what you think the act of swallowing a bird represents in the poem.
2. The man is changed by having "swallowed a bird." What new qualities does the speaker observe in him in stanza three?

3. The man's friends do not understand what has happened to him. What lines or phrases show their puzzlement and uneasiness? Why is it appropriate that stanza four, in which the changed man speaks, is set off from the others?

4. The man explains, in stanza four, that the experience at first made him feel "like a cage," but that feeling gave way to joy. We also know that "The change took time" (stanza two). What do these observations imply about the growth of a person's spirit? Is the process difficult? effortless? confining? liberating? painful? rewarding?

5. His new knowledge and freedom bring the man joy but also restlessness (line 12). One day (line 18) he vanishes (or can no longer be understood or "seen" by ordinary people), leaving only "odd songs" which remind others of him. Does the poet seem to be saying that in absorbing this spirit one cannot remain part of the human community? or that most people simply cannot comprehend such growth of spirit?

Composition

Write a short story, poem, or essay in which a person is changed physically to reflect some change in his or her character. Make the change in appearance appropriate for the kind of change in personality. Try to indicate how the people who see the change react to it.

Compare and Contrast

In both "The Man Who Swallowed a Bird" and "The Tuft of Flowers" a person attains a feeling of oneness with nature. In what way is the feeling of the two people for the natural world the same? Because of the experience, both feel a new relationship to other people. How is this relationship different in the two poems?

DAVID WAGONER
(born 1926)

Ohio-born David Wagoner received a B.A. from Pennsylvania State University in 1947 and an M.A. from Indiana University in 1949. Although he has taught at several universities, Wagoner has taught since 1954 at the University of Washington in Seattle. He has received a number of fellowships and grants, and has edited the magazine *Poetry Northwest* since 1966.

Besides having published nine books of poems, Wagoner has written seven novels and a play. He has also edited the notebooks of Theodor Roethke (see the biographical sketch on page 32), who was his teacher and later a colleague, and who had a strong influence on Wagoner's work.

Wagoner's poems have been called by one critic "among the most moving and delightful things recent culture has given us." The poems are made with the intensity and dexterity of language that poetry demands. They are also richly inventive—that is, they have a power to express relationships and ideas in new, engaging ways—without being merely clever. As poet James Dickey has noted, they often combine "abandon, wild calculation and seriousness" in a way that both pulls the reader's leg and shows the truth of the condition Wagoner describes.

The Man Who Spilled Light

The man who spilled light wasn't to blame for it.
He was in a hurry to bring it home to the city
Where, everyone said, there was too much darkness:
"Look at those shadows," they said. "They're dangerous.
5   Who's there? What's that?" and crouching,
     "Who are *you?*"
So he went and scraped up all the light he could find.

But it was too much to handle and started spilling:
Flakes and star-marks, shafts of it splitting
To ring-light and light gone slack or jagged,

10   Clouds folded inside out, whole pools
      And hummocks° and domes of light,
      Egg-light, light tied in knots or peeled in swatches,°
      Daylight as jumbled as jackstraws° falling.

      Then everything seemed perfectly obvious
15   Wherever they looked. There was nothing
          they couldn't see.
      The corners and alleys all looked empty,
      And no one could think of anything terrible
      Except behind their backs, so they all lined up
      With their backs to walls and felt perfectly fine.
20   And the man who'd spilled it felt fine for a while,
      But then he noticed people squinting.

      They should have been looking at everything,
          and everything
      Should have been perfectly clear, and everyone
      Should have seemed perfectly brilliant, there was
          so much
25   Dazzle: people were dazzled, they were dazzling,
      But they were squinting, trying to make darkness
      All over again in the cracks between their eyelids.
      So he swept up all the broken light
      For pity's sake and put it back where it came from.

11. **hummocks:** hills or knolls.   12. **swatches:** samples of cloth;
patches.   13. **jackstraws:** narrow strips of wood used in playing a
game called pick-up-sticks.

Meaning and Method

1. What did the people fear that made them want more light?
   How do you think they believed the light would help?
2. Light enables us to see physical objects, but as a symbol light
   represents understanding. People fear darkness, or what they
   don't know or "see," because it may contain something threatening. How does the sentence, "There was nothing they
   couldn't see" (line 15), apply both literally (in ordinary meaning) and symbolically to the people who received light?

3. What descriptive words or phrases in stanza two show that the light was made up of a jumble of all kinds of light that refused to mix? Why might the man have been unable to handle it?
4. With the light released, "everything seemed perfectly obvious" (line 14). Why, then, did the people line up with their backs to the wall before they could feel "perfectly fine" (line 19)?
5. The poet implies that in order to bring total "light" to people, it had to be "jumbled" (line 13) unnaturally and "broken" (line 28); the people were not content with the perfect brilliance and tried to "make darkness/All over again" (lines 26–27) by squinting. In what way do you think the light was too much for the human race to handle? What do you think the poem shows about the limits of human nature? the ability of people to see and understand everything?

TONE

When someone speaks, the *tone* of voice he or she uses communicates the attitude with which the words are spoken. For instance, when your mother says, "No, you cannot go," the tone in which she says it tells you immediately whether it will do you any good to plead now or ask again later. The tone of a poem is the attitude of its speaker. When we read a poem, we do not have the advantage of hearing the words spoken, but the tone is communicated by the overall effect which poetic devices give the poem. The images, figures of speech, connotations, rhythm, format, sentence construction, etc., work together to create a sense of the speaker's attitude.

In "The Lake of Innisfree" (p. 16), Yeats's use of the long, slow lines, peaceful images, and smooth, flowing sounds builds a tone of quiet longing for that environment while the speaker stands "on the pavements gray." The long lines broken by exclamation marks and dashes, the fierceness of the figures of speech, the sentences constructed in terse commands in Whitman's "Beat! Beat! Drums!" (p. 53) all work together to create a tone of solemn sorrow for the ruthless force of war.

Just as we do not know how to react to someone's words until we take into account the tone in which they were spoken, so we do not fully understand a poem until we can grasp the attitude of its speaker, shown in the poem's tone.

DAVID DAICHES*
(born 1912)

David Daiches was born in 1912 in Sunderland, England, but grew up in Edinburgh, Scotland, where his father was a rabbi and leader of the Scottish Jewish community. He showed himself to be an exceptional student from an early age, and won first-class honors when he was graduated from Edinburgh University. At the age of twenty-four, he received a doctorate from Balliol College, Oxford.

Today Daiches is well known in both Great Britain and the United States as a professor of English literature and as a creative scholar and critic. In the many critical books he has written since 1936, he has revealed a broad interest in and insight into both English and American literature of the past and of the contemporary scene.

Daiches' scholarly successes did not turn him into a pompous academic. He has always had a lively interest in both the world around him and the world of words. His interest in the latter is shown not only in his prose but also in his light verse.

* **Daiches** (dā'chəz).

Thoughts on Progress

In days of old when knights caught cold,
They were not quickly cured;
No aspirin pill would check the ill,
Which had to be endured.

5   You sat it out if toothache hurt you;
Patience was esteemed a virtue.

The dentist's way in Hogarth's° day
Was pretty rough and ready;
His foot he'd rest on patient's breast
10   To keep his pincers° steady,

7. Hogarth: a seventeenth-century English illustrator who caricatured the social and political life of his time. **10. pincers** (pin'sərz): an instrument used for gripping things; for example, pliers.

And if the dentist's patient screamed,
The dentist was the more esteemed.

De Quincey's° age could well assuage°
Some kinds of pain and grief;
15   To bard° in bed with aching head
Laudanum° gave relief,
And sometimes in the process brought
A quickening of poetic thought.

When chloroform became the norm
20   For those who faced the surgeon,
A man or wife would meet the knife
Without excessive urgin',
And dentists learned to stop the pain
With useful things like novocain.

25   The anesthetic's with us yet,
And so's the analgesic,°
And dramamine° relieves the keen
Afflictions of the seasick.
And we've new blessings for the ill in
30   Sulfa drugs and penicillin.

When modern wight° retires at night
With streptomycin handy,
He finds repose at once; he knows
That everything is dandy.
35   No fear of sudden plague will keep
The trustful modern from his sleep.

Yet pharmacists have got long lists
Of pills that hasten slumber,
And they report that of that sort
40   They sell a shocking number,

13. **De Quincey:** nineteenth-century English writer, author of *Confessions of an English Opium Eater;*   **assuage** (ǝ·swāj′)**:** to lessen or diminish.   **15. bard:** poet, particularly one who writes about historic and legendary events.   **16. Laudanum:** an opium drug.   **26. analgesic** (an′ǝl·jē′zik)**:** a pain-killing drug.   **27. dramamine** (dram′ǝ·mēn)**.**   **31. wight:** an archaic word meaning "person."

For somehow still we cannot find,
It seems, a settled peace of mind.

Try, try again, you medicine men!
The riddle's tough and bitter;
45 We've got the drugs that kill the bugs
But still we tense and jitter.
Ancestral terrors haunt us still—
Anxiety, where is thy pill?

fear of death

Meaning and Method

1. The speaker describes "progress" in medical and dental prac-
tice, noting particularly the invention of drugs which reduce
pain. What specific changes does he mention? According to the
speaker, what have new inventions not been able to do? In your
answer, explain the meaning of *ancestral terrors* (line 47).

2. *Satire* is a method of criticism in which vice or folly is made to
seem ridiculous. Is this poem a satire on medicine? on the idea
of progress? something else? In your answer, comment on the
connotations of such expressions as *trustful modern* (line 36) and
medicine men (line 43).

3. One way in which Daiches creates a humorous tone is through
his use of unexpected rhymes, as in "hurt you/virtue" (lines 5
and 6). What other rhymes do you consider humorous? Note
that several of the humorous rhymes appear as *rhymed couplets* at
the end of each stanza—that is, as two successive lines of verse
with the same rhyming sound. Besides his use of rhyme, how
does Daiches achieve a humorous tone?

Language: How Scientific and Medical Terms Are Formed

If you had invented a new product, one of the first things you
would do would be to try to think of a name for it. You might
make up the name out of random sounds or from a random
combination of words. However, if you were seriously thinking of
a name for your product, you would be more likely to describe it
by combining existing words, or Latin and Greek roots of words.

The latter method is the one most often used in forming new scientific and medical words. For example, when its discoverer wanted to describe the fungus (a low form of plant life) which eventually produced penicillin, he called it Penicillium from the Latin *penicillus,* or paintbrush, because the tufts of the fungus resembled a paintbrush. When its discoverer wanted to describe the moldlike organism from which we get the drug streptomycin, he took the Greek roots *streptos,* which means "twisted," and *mykus,* which means "fungus," to describe the way the organism looked and to denote its place in the plant kingdom.

Many other scientific and medical terms were formed from Latin and Greek roots. Among these are the following:

1. radium
2. telescope
3. seismograph
4. antihistamine
5. Terramycin
6. asthma
7. poliomyelitis
8. tuberculosis

Look up the origins of these words in a dictionary and be prepared to explain why the roots of these words give some indication of the meanings of the words.

Discussion and Composition

1. In his final stanza, Daiches stresses the presence of anxiety in modern life. Another poet, W. H. Auden, has written a long dramatic poem on this subject, entitled *The Age of Anxiety.* Do you think ours is an "age of anxiety"? Is the phrase a more appropriate description of our era than of past eras? In a panel discussion, explain your viewpoint.

2. Since Daiches wrote this poem, tranquilizers, which are drugs to relieve feelings of anxiety, have become popular. Write one stanza containing three rhymed couplets beginning with the line: "Anxiety, you have your pill."

PHYLLIS McGINLEY
(born 1905)

In situations where other people see only irritation, Phyllis McGinley points out humor. Her special province is Suburbia—the world of homemakers, commuting spouses, assorted children, and domestic problems. Instead of bemoaning the fate of the suburban woman or complaining about boredom, McGinley, with controlled irony and an easy mastery of poetic technique, makes the reader laugh. As a result, she has become one of the most popular poets in the United States, and is the particular favorite of tens of thousands of housewives who ordinarily feel forgotten and misunderstood.

Miss McGinley, who was born in Oregon, is herself a suburban wife and the mother of two grown daughters. However, the Pulitzer Prize winner does not like to be thought of as a housewife who is also a poet. In support of her contention, she could point to the fact that her first book of poems was published in 1934, three years before she married Charles Hayden and settled in Larchmont, New York. She could also point out that many of her poems and essays are concerned with the general foibles of people in the twentieth century. Nevertheless, her experiences as a wife and mother have given her most of her material for her poetry. In her most characteristic poems, her heroine is a housewife attempting to battle the enemies of order and sanity with a sense of humor.

Season at the Shore

Oh, not by sun and not by cloud
And not by whippoorwill, crying loud,
And not by the pricking of my thumbs,
Do I know the way that the summer comes.
5   Yet here on this seagull-haunted strand,
Hers is an omen I understand—
Sand:

Sand on the beaches,
    Sand at the door,
10   Sand that screeches
    On the new-swept floor;
In the shower, sand for the foot to crunch on;
Sand in the sandwiches spread for luncheon;
Sand adhesive to son and sibling,°
15   From wallet sifting, from pockets dribbling;
Sand by the beaker°
    Nightly shed
From odious sneaker;
    Sand in bed;
20   Sahara always in my seaside shanty
Like the sand in the voice
Of J. Durante.°

Winter is mittens, winter is gaiters°
Steaming on various radiators.
25   Autumn is leaves that bog the broom.
Spring is mud in the living room
Or skates in places one scarcely planned.
But what is summer, her seal and hand?
Sand:

30   Sand in the closets,
    Sand on the stair,
Desert deposits
    In the parlor chair;
Sand in the halls like the halls of ocean;
35   Sand in the soap and the sun-tan lotion;
Stirred in the porridge, tossed in the greens,
Poured from the bottoms of rolled-up jeans;
    In the elmy street
      On the lawny acre;
40   Glued to the seat
      Of the Studebaker;°

14. sibling: a sister or brother. **16. beaker:** a large, wide-mouthed goblet. **22. J. Durante:** Jimmy Durante, a singer-comedian famous for his large nose and gravelly voice. **23. gaiters:** *here,* leggings. **41. Studebaker:** an automobile which is no longer made in the United States.

Wrapped in the folds of the *Wall Street Journal;*
Damp sand, dry sand,
Sand eternal.
45   When I shake my garments at the Lord's command,
What will I scatter in the Promised Land?
Sand.

Meaning and Method

1. How does the speaker's way of defining the seasons in lines 23–29 show that she is a housewife and a mother?
2. One humorous technique used in this poem is that of leading up to a point and then giving a totally unexpected answer or example. Where has Phyllis McGinley used this technique? Explain your answers with examples from the poem.
3. Why does the poet use the /s/ sound throughout the poem? Find several examples of this technique.
4. Many rhymes seem connected to each other by meaning as well as sound. For example, *moon* and *June* both have romantic connotations. Phyllis McGinley, however, deliberately uses rhymes which seem incongruous or out of place. For example, she rhymes the word *sibling*—a word more often seen in textbooks than heard in informal speech—with *dribbling.* In what other rhymes has she mixed levels of vocabulary, or used surprising combinations?

Composition

1. Write a humorous composition about homework in which you exaggerate the amount and type your teachers give you. However, write the composition as if you were complaining seriously.

2. Characterize one of the seasons humorously in prose (or in poetry), much as Phyllis McGinley has done in lines **23–29.** Use details which give your impression of the season.

WILLIAM BLAKE
(1757–1827)

Even as a boy William Blake exhibited the sensitive nature and original talent that made him a great artist and poet. His terror and outrage over discipline led his parents to let Blake study at home. He studied what he liked, mostly literature and art, and by the age of ten had shown such promise that he was sent to art school. The visionary aspect of Blake's personality was also evident early in his life. He saw visions that convinced him of the reality of the spiritual in humankind. To illustrate, on one of Blake's frequent walks in the countryside near London, the seven-year-old boy saw a tree full of angels.

Blake called this world "a world of imagination and vision." Throughout his life, his philosophy and work hinged on a belief that any person could "see" as he did with the use of the God-given creative imagination. To him it was obvious that the outward physical object is not as real as the spiritual aspect that the object represents.

Blake's work allowed for, even celebrated, the existence of opposite qualities within the human being. Two of his best-known works, *Songs of Innocence* and *Songs of Experience*, balance one another by showing the balance in people of what Blake called "contraries" (opposites) of human nature. A capacity for joyful innocence exists along with darker, but no less valid, capacities that come with experience. In these poems, Blake's heavy use of symbolism can be appreciated. The poems rarely consider an object as itself alone, but rather as some aspect of the spirit, which it represents. "The Lamb," one of the poems Blake addressed to children, is taken from *Songs of Innocence*.

The Lamb

Little Lamb, who made thee?
Dost thou know who made thee?
Gave thee life, and bid thee feed,
By the stream and o'er the mead;

5   Gave thee clothing of delight,
Softest clothing, woolly, bright;
Gave thee such a tender voice,
Making all the vales rejoice?
     Little Lamb, who made thee?
10   Dost thou know who made thee?

     Little Lamb, I'll tell thee,
     Little Lamb, I'll tell thee;
He is callèd by thy name,
For he calls himself a Lamb:
15   He is meek, and he is mild,
He became a little child:
I a child, and thou a lamb,
We are callèd by his name.
     Little Lamb, God bless thee!
20   Little Lamb, God bless thee!

Meaning and Method

1. The first stanza asks a question and in the process describes the lamb. How does the speaker view the lamb?
2. In the answer (second stanza) the speaker identifies the lamb and the child (himself) with the maker. Who is the maker? How does this identification help explain the joyous tone of the poem? Why is the speaker happy?
3. Why do you think Blake repeated certain lines and phrases, for example, the first two lines of the second stanza? Does the repetition in any way reinforce the attitude of childlike delight?

STEVIE SMITH
(1902–1971)

Florence Margaret Smith was nicknamed "Stevie" after a well-known jockey because of her small size. She grew up in a London suburb and was early employed in a London publishing house as a secretary. She resigned this job, however, in order to care for a bed-ridden aunt.

Her poetry is unclassifiable and original. Several critics have likened her to Emily Dickinson. Certain themes recur: loneliness, death, and people in peculiar circumstances—a drowning man, a dying woman who is the end of a long line of Roman citizens.

Smith was a popular reader of her own poems at schools and universities. She wrote three novels as well as nine books of verse, among them, *A Good Time Was Had By All* (1937), *Tender Only to One* (1938), *Mother What Is Man* (1942), *Harold's Leap* (1950), *Not Waving but Drowning* (1959), *Selected Poems* (1962), *Frog Prince* (1966), and *Scorpion and Other Poems* (1971).

The Boat

The boat that took my love away
He sent again to me
To tell me that he would not sleep
Alone beneath the sea.

5   The flower and fruit of love are mine
The ant, the fieldmouse and the mole,
But now a tiger prowls without
And claws upon my soul.

Love is not love that wounded bleeds
10   And bleeding sullies slow.
Come death within my hands and I
Unto my love will go.

Meaning and Method

1. In Blake's poem "The Lamb," the lamb comes to represent both the child and his maker. What might the boat represent in this poem?
2. The tiger in this poem is contrasted with the ant, the fieldmouse and the mole. What might they each represent?

Compare and Contrast

1. "Love is not love" in line 9 is a reference to Shakespeare's Sonnet 116. The complete sentence in Shakespeare is "Love is not love/which alters when it alteration finds/Or bends with the re-mover to remove." How does this literary allusion (see Glossary) add to the meaning of this poem?
2. Compare "The Boat" with Emily Dickinson's "The Wind Tapped Like a Tired Man" (page 41). Pay particular attention to the choice of words, rhyme scheme, and personification.

THEODORE ROETHKE

A biographical sketch of Theodore Roethke appears on page 32.

The Sloth

In moving-slow he has no Peer.
You ask him something in his ear;
He thinks about it for a Year;

And, then, before he says a Word
5   There, upside down (unlike a Bird)
He will assume that you have Heard—

A most Ex-as-per-at-ing Lug.
But should you call his manner Smug,
He'll sigh and give his Branch a Hug;

10   Then off again to Sleep he goes,
Still swaying gently by his Toes,
And you just *know* he knows he knows.

Meaning and Method

1. In the poem, Roethke has pictured characteristic traits of the sloth (sluggish movement and the habit of hanging from tree branches). With what details has he also created a personality for the sloth? Note especially lines 3, 6, and 8–9 in forming your answer. Describe its personality in your own words.
2. What pattern of rhyme is used? How might the effect of a triple rhyme help create a humorous tone?
3. How does the hyphenation of *exasperating* in line 7 indicate the speaker's annoyance? In the last line, what does the speaker *know* the sloth knows? How do the italicized word and the repetition of "he knows" add to the speaker's exasperated tone?

Composition

Write a poem or essay in which you describe an encounter with another wild animal, such as an alligator or a whale. Assume that the animal can understand and reply to you. Create physical and/or spoken responses that will show the character you associate with the animal.

ALFRED, LORD TENNYSON
(1809–1892)

As a child growing up in a country parsonage in England, Alfred Tennyson showed both talent for and devotion to poetry. Before he was fifteen, he had written two verse plays, a 6,000-line narrative poem, and many shorter poems.

Although the poems came easily, success for Tennyson as a poet came hard. For years he fought the criticism of reviewers, financial problems, and, most important, his own grief over the loss of his fellow student and dearest friend.

After Arthur Henry Hallam died in 1833, Tennyson devoted himself to writing poems telling of his grief and the religious doubts caused by Hallam's death, and of his final resignation and faith. When these poems were published in 1850 under the title *In Memoriam,* they gained Tennyson great popularity, financial success (allowing him to marry his fiancée of twelve years), and appointment by Queen Victoria as Poet Laureate of England.

Tennyson had a gift for creating tender, dreamlike lyrics, and an ability to mirror the ideas of his time in characters drawn from legend or his own imagination. These qualities made him so popular in later life that he received honors usually granted to those who had performed unusual public services. He was made a baron in 1883, and took a seat in the House of Lords. When he died, he was given the rare tribute of a funeral in Westminster Abbey in London. Though some of his poetry is shallow and sentimental, both the people and the governments of his time showed good judgment: for his best work, Tennyson ranks among the greatest English poets.

Break, Break, Break

Break, break, break
   On thy cold grey stones, O Sea!
And I would that my tongue could utter
   The thoughts that arise in me.

5 O, well for the fisherman's boy,
       That he shouts with his sister at play!
   O, well for the sailor lad,
       That he sings in his boat on the bay!

   And the stately ships go on
10   To their haven° under the hill;
   But O for the touch of a vanished hand,
       And the sound of a voice that is still!

   Break, break, break
       At the foot of thy crags, O sea!
15 But the tender grace of a day that is dead
       Will never come back to me.

   10. haven: a port; also, a shelter or safe place.

Meaning and Method

1. A poem written to mourn the death of a specific person is called
   an *elegy*. The elegy may emphasize grief at this individual death,
   or it may treat the death as an occasion to lament the passing of
   beauty and life in general. Most elegies are long, formal poems
   of a meditative nature. However, they can also be short lyrics,
   as is this poem which Tennyson wrote after the death of his
   friend, Arthur Henry Hallam. The speaker grieves for a "voice
   that is still," and his own voice cannot utter his thoughts (lines
   3–4). What contrast do the voices of the children in stanza two
   present? Why do they disturb him? Why do the sounds of
   the sea seem like a voice to him now?

2. How is the breaking of the sea on the rocks like the "breaking"
   of a human life (that is, dying)? How is it different? Do you
   think the speaker envies the sea for being eternal? Why might
   the poet have repeated *break* three times (lines 1 and 13) instead
   of just saying *Break on thy cold grey stones?*

3. Is the speaker mourning only for the loss of his friend, or for the
   loss of his youth as well? Explain your answer, using lines 15–16
   and showing how they contrast with lines 5–10.

4. Is the tone of the poem one of envy? sorrow? Point out some details and devices (like stanza pattern and rhythm) which help establish the tone.

Compare and Contrast

In both "The Sloth" and "Break, Break, Break" regular patterns of rhythm, rhyme, and stanza form are used, but create very different moods. How do these patterns differ? How do the differences in the way rhyme, rhythm, and stanza form are used establish different moods?

The Kinds of Poetry

NARRATIVE POETRY

Poetry did not begin as a written art form enjoyed by only a few. Early *narrative,* or story, poems grew out of the need of whole nations of people for entertainment (song) and for a means of "recording" and transmitting accounts of things that concerned them. Before writing and printing became common, narrative poems were often composed and sung by ordinary, uneducated persons. Many of these brief story-songs, or *folk ballads,* composed centuries ago by unknown people, were passed down for generations by word of mouth and are still sung today. Different versions came into being as individual singers introduced changes in the years before ballads were written down. Professional poet-singers called minstrels sang these ballads for eager audiences,* but they cannot truly be called the poets of these ballads, for it was the common people who passed the stories down generation after generation, elaborating on them as they worked or relaxed together, making the ballad a form that belongs to the people.

Because the ballad was an oral form intended for group participation, it was necessarily direct and simple. Ballads tended to relate only the most important details of plot in as dramatic a way as possible. This made memorization easier. They also used commonplace language with which everyone in the audience was familiar. A repeated line or refrain gave listeners a chance to join their voices. The principal singer would not treat the theme in a personal way, for everyone in the audience had to respond to what was sung.

Folk ballads served as a sort of news medium, recording crimes and tragic or shocking stories, important historic events, even "news" of the visits of supernatural creatures. Some ballads

---

* Bards composed and sang extremely long story-poems, or *folk epics.* Because the epic is a complex literary type, it is treated separately in another section.

helped create legends out of actual events, as in the case of Robin Hood. Ballad audiences also wanted to hear tragic love stories about lovers who came from powerful families (as in "The Douglas Tragedy" on page 95 and in "Lord Randal" on page 102) or humorous stories about incidents in the lives of ordinary couples (as in "Get Up and Bar the Door" on page 105).

Folk ballads have had great literary influence. When writing and printing became common, writers not only set the current versons of ballads to paper, but also adapted the techniques and characteristics of the original folk type, thus creating *literary epics* and *literary ballads*. ("Proud Maisie" on page 112 is one example; "Old Christmas," p. 115, is another.) Since these forms are communicated through print rather than song, they tend toward greater complexity of language and detail.

We are not certain how long ago people began composing and singing ballads. The oldest English folk ballads we know of originated at least five or six centuries ago in England and Scotland. Many were brought to America by colonial settlers, who often adapted them to fit the conditions of American life.

Many more ballads sprang out of the experiences of American settlers, slaves, and workers. Native American ballads frequently share the same general subjects found in English and Scottish ballads. One element which distinguishes the American ballad, however, is the type of character it celebrates. While an English ballad often sings of lords and ladies—aristocratic people—dying tragically, the American ballad sings of people who earn their own livings by fair means or foul—lumberjacks, cowboys, railroad men, gamblers—and who are often capable of superhuman feats (for example, "John Henry" on page 108). While they often tell sad love stories, American folk song stories are seldom deeply tragic. In fact, they are likely to show a lighthearted or determined attitude, reflecting the spirit of a pioneer people who refused to let their troubles defeat them.

Besides the narrative poems in the oral tradition of the ballad, other types have been written more recently. These often combine the techniques of the ballad with those of lyric poetry.

Long or short, all narrative poems tell a story, combining action and the musical elements of poetry in very satisfying ways.

The Douglas Tragedy

There are many versions of this ballad, but they all concern a certain family in Selkirkshire, in the Border Country of Scotland. The lovers in the poem, Lord William and Lady Margaret, were probably members of feuding clans, groups of families, each of which claimed a common ancestor.

"Rise up, rise up now, Lord Douglas," she says,
   "And put on your armor so bright;
Let it never be said that a daughter of thine
   Was married to a lord under night.°

5   "Rise up, rise up, my seven bold sons,
   And put on your armor so bright,
And take better care o' your youngest sister,
   For your eldest's away the last night."

He's° mounted her on a milk-white steed,
10   And himself on a dapple gray,
With a bugelet° horn hung down by his side,
   And lightly they rode away.

Lord William lookit o'er his left shoulder,
   To see what he could see,
15   And there he spied her seven brethren bold,
   Come riding o'er the lee.°

"Light down,° light down, Lady Margaret," he said,
   "And hold my steed in your hand,
Until that against your seven brethren bold,
20   And your father, I make a stand."

She held his steed in her milk-white hand,
   And never shed one tear,

4. married . . . under night: eloped under cover of the night.
9. He's: refers to Lord William, the lover who eloped with Lord Douglas' daughter. **11. bugelet:** small bugle. **16. lee:** a place protected from the wind; probably a hillside. **17. Light down:** alight, get down.

Until that she saw her seven brethren fall,
    And her father hard-fighting, who loved her so dear.

25   "O hold your hand, Lord William!" she said,
    "For your strokes they are wondrous sore;°
True lovers I can get many a one,
    But a father I can never get more."

O she's ta'en out her handkerchief,
30   It was o' the Holland° so fine,
And aye° she dighted° her father's bloody wounds,
    That were redder than the wine.

"O choose, O choose, Lady Margaret," he said,
    "O whether will ye gang or bide?"°
35   "I'll gang, I'll gang, Lord William," she said,
    "For ye have left me no other guide."

He's lifted her on a milk-white steed.
    And himself on a dapple gray,
With a bugelet horn hung down by his side,
40   And slowly they both rode away.

O they rode on, and on they rode,
    And all by the light o' the moon,
Until they came to yon wan water,°
    And there they lighted down.

45   They lighted down to take a drink
    O' the spring that ran so clear
And down the stream ran his good heart's blood,
    And sore° she 'gan to fear.

"Hold up, hold up, Lord William," she says,
50   "For I fear that you are slain."

26. sore: painful, severe.   **30. Holland:** a fine fabric originally made
in the Netherlands.   **31. aye** (ī): continually;   **dighted:** wiped.
34. gang or bide: go or stay.   **43. yon wan water:** yonder pale
water. The original singer was describing a place his listeners knew.
48. sore: greatly.

"'Tis nothing but the shadow o' my scarlet cloak,
   That shines in the water so plain."

O they rode on, and on they rode,
   And all by the light o' the moon
55 Until they came to his mother's hall° door,
   And there they lighted down.

"Get up, get up, lady mother," he says,
   "Get up and let me in!
Get up, get up, lady mother," he says,
60   "For this night my fair lady I've win.

"O make my bed,° lady mother," he says,
   "O make it broad and deep,
And lay Lady Margaret close at my back,
   And the sounder I will sleep."

65 Lord William was dead long ere° midnight,
   Lady Margaret long ere day,
And all true lovers that go together,
   May they have more luck than they!

Lord William was buried in St. Mary's kirk,°
70   Lady Margaret in Mary's quire;°
Out o' the lady's grave grew a bonny red rose,
   And out o' the knight's a briar.

And they two met, and they two plat,°
   And fain° they would be near;
75 And all the world might ken° right well°
   They were two lovers dear.

---

55. hall: castle. **61. make my bed:** In folk ballads, this request is
usually a preparation for death. **65. ere:** before. **69. kirk:** church.
70. quire: variation for the word choir. In old English churches, the
choir was near the altar, separating the sanctuary from the congregation. **71-73. red rose . . . plat:** Plat means intertwined. The image of
a rose and a briar growing out of the lovers' graves and forming a
lover's knot is a standard ballad image. **74. fain:** willingly.
75. ken: know; **right well:** without doubt.

Meaning and Method

1. Who is the speaker in the first two stanzas? How do you know? Why is the speaker disturbed?
2. Describe Lady Margaret's attitude before and after the fight. Why does it change? How does the fight affect her feeling for Lord William? In your answer explain why the lovers ride "lightly" in line 12 and "slowly" in line 40.
3. The few details given have meaningful connotations. What are the connotations of **a.** the colors of the lovers' horses and **b.** the color of Lord William's cloak? Why are they significant? What is the significance of the fact that the action takes place at night?
4. From dialogue and action, how would you characterize Lord William? Lady Margaret? For example, what is shown about Lord William by his lying to Lady Margaret about his blood in the water?

Language: Origins of Names

Last names usually have origins that can be traced to an occupation or place of birth. The name "Douglas," for example, which comes from the Gaelic *dubh glas* ("dark water"), indicates that the first Douglases probably lived near a muddy or dark river or lake.

Besides Douglas, other names which refer to features of a landscape are Brooks, Hill, Marsh, and Woods. Many other names, such as Baker, Butler, or Miller, originally reflected occupations. Still other names were derived from colors—for example, Brown, Rossi ("red" in Italian), Schwartz ("black" in German)—and from physical characteristics—for example, Small and Klein ("little" in German). How many other names can you think of which reflect places of birth, occupation, colors, or physical characteristics?

First names also have meanings. In a dictionary, find the origin and meaning of your first name, and be prepared to explain it in class.

Barbara Allen

Many ballads originating in England and Scotland were brought to America by the early settlers. "Barbara Allen," one of the most popular, exists in more than a hundred versions. Here is a Scottish version.

It was in and about the Martinmas° time,
   When the green leaves were a-fallin',
That Sir John Graeme in the West Country
   Fell in love with Barbara Allen.°

5 He sent his man down through the town
      To the place where she was dwellin':
   "O haste and come to my master dear,
      Gin° ye be Barbara Allen."

   O slowly, slowly rase° she up,
10   To the place where he was lyin',
   And when she drew the curtain by:
      "Young man, I think you're dyin'."

   "O it's I'm sick, and very, very sick,
      And 'tis a' for Barbara Allen."
15 "O the better for me ye sal° never be,
      Though your heart's blood were a-spillin'.

   "O dinna ye mind,° young man," said she,
      "When ye the cups were fillin',
   That ye made the healths° gae round and round,
20   And slighted Barbara Allen?"

   He turned his face unto the wall,
      And death with him was dealin':

1. Martinmas: also spelled Martinmass; November 11th, the feast of St. Martin of Tours, a day of harvest and thanksgiving celebration. **4. Barbara Allen:** also spelled Barbra Allen, or Barbara Allan. **8. Gin:** if. **9. rase:** rose. **15. sal:** shall. **17. dinna ye mind:** don't you remember. **19. healths:** toasts to prosperity or good health.

"Adieu,° adieu, my dear friends all,
    And be kind to Barbara Allen."

25 And slowly, slowly, rase she up,
        And slowly, slowly left him;
    And sighing said she could not stay,
        Since death of life had reft° him.

    She had not gane a mile but twa,°
30   When she heard the dead-bell knellin',
    And every jow° that the dead-bell ga'ed°
        It cried, "Woe to Barbara Allen!"

    "O mother, mother, make my bed,
        O make it soft and narrow:
35 Since my love died for me today,
        I'll die for him tomorrow."

23. Adieu (ə·dōō′): goodbye. **28. reft:** deprived. **29. not ...
twa:** gone only two miles. **31. jow:** stroke; **ga'ed:** gave.

Meaning and Method

1. Why does Barbara scorn her love? Why does she undergo a
   change of heart after Sir John dies? Did Barbara love the dead
   man? In your answer, discuss her final speech.
2. A *theme* is the main idea or one of the ideas developed in a
   poem, story, or essay. What is the theme of this version of
   "Barbara Allen"?
3. Most ballads are composed in *ballad stanzas*—that is, four-line
   stanzas with the last words of the second and fourth lines rhyming. The *rhyme scheme,* or pattern of rhymed lines, is therefore
   abcb (*b* represents the two rhymed sounds; *a* and *c,* the
   unrhymed sounds). The meter of the ballad stanzas consists of
   an alternation of four stressed syllables in one line with three
   stressed syllables in the next. Be able to explain these specific
   characteristics of the ballad by pointing out examples in the
   stanzas of "Barbara Allen."

Language: Dialects

When Barbara Allen says, "dinna ye mind," she is speaking in the Scottish *dialect,* a variation of standard English in which pronunciations and expressions peculiar to the Scots are used. Dialects most often develop when one part of a country is relatively isolated. However, even when the original cause of isolation—for example, the difficulty of traveling long distances—has been overcome, dialects continue to be spoken. One generation passes on its way of speaking to the next.

Some examples of dialect used in poetry are:

1. "I got wings, you got wings,
   All God's chillun got wings;
   When I git to Heb'n goin' to put on my wings. . . ."
   American Negro spiritual, "All God's Chillun" (*Southern Negro dialect*)
2. "How can ye chant, ye little birds,
   And I sae fu' o' care. . . ."
   Robert Burns, "The Banks o' Doon" (*Scottish dialect*)
3. "He mowed all day. At last he feels
   A pisen sarpent bite his heels."
   Traditional ballad, "Springfield Mountain" (*Appalachian mountain dialect*)

Rewrite these verses in standard English.

Composition

Take a story from a newspaper that you think might make a good ballad. Rewrite the story in your own words in one paragraph. In a second paragraph, explain why you have chosen it. In a concluding paragraph, tell what parts of the story you would emphasize if you were writing a ballad, and give reasons for your choices.

Lord Randal

In this ballad, the dialogue between a nobleman and his mother slowly reveals a tragedy.

"O where hae° ye been, Lord Randal my son?
O where hae ye been, my handsome young man?"
   "I hae been to the wild wood; mother, make my bed
     soon,
   For I'm weary wi' hunting, and fain wald° lie down."

5   "Where got ye your dinner, Lord Randal my son?
Where got ye your dinner, my handsome young man?"
   "I dined wi' my true-love; mother, make my bed
     soon,
   For I'm weary wi' hunting, and fain wald lie down."

"What got ye to your dinner, Lord Randal my son?
10   What got ye to your dinner, my handsome young man?"
   "I got eels boiled in broo;° mother, make my bed
     soon,
   For I'm weary wi' hunting, and fain wald lie down."

"What became of your bloodhounds, Lord Randal
     my son?
What became of your bloodhounds, my handsome
     young man?"
15   "O they swelled and they died; mother, make my bed
     soon,
   For I'm weary wi' hunting, and fain wald lie down."

"O I fear ye are poisoned, Lord Randal my son!
O I fear ye are poisoned, my handsome young man!"
   "O yes, I am poisoned; mother, make my bed soon,
20   For I'm sick at the heart, and I fain wald lie down,"

1. hae: have.   **4. fain wald:** gladly would.   **11. broo:** broth.

Meaning and Method

1. What facts does the mother know about Lord Randal before she begins questioning him? What does she suspect? Which question indicates that the mother realizes what has happened? Give reasons for your answers.
2. Why, in your opinion, does Lord Randal not immediately tell his mother that he has been poisoned? Why does he call the girl who poisoned him his "true-love"? In what ways is he "sick at the heart"?
3. Repetition, a common ballad technique, is used to characterize the mother. What characteristic is shown by her repetition of questions? Is repetition used to characterize Lord Randal? to emphasize the meaning of his words? for some other reason?
4. The story is told entirely by means of questions and answers. Why does this method arouse the curiosity of the reader? Is there anything you need to know that has not been told?

Language: Origins of the English Language

A language, like a person or a nation, does not develop overnight. The English language took many centuries to reach its present state and, like all living languages, it is constantly changing.

The first major stage through which the English language passed is now known as Old English or Anglo-Saxon, since the language was derived from the dialects spoken by the Angles, Saxons, and other Germanic tribes who migrated to England in the fifth and sixth centuries A.D. Though Old English now seems like a foreign language to us, many of our basic words, such as *child, life, house, speak, old, bone, boat,* and *meat,* are derived from it. Words derived from Anglo-Saxon or Old English are usually short, concrete words.

The second major stage in the development of the English language began after William the Conqueror's successful invasion of England in 1066. William came from a part of France known as Normandy and spoke in a language we now refer to as Old French.

For almost two centuries after the conquest, Old French was the primary language of the government, clergy, and nobles in England. It was not until the end of the thirteenth century that English had strongly reestablished itself. However, thirteenth-century English, or Middle English, was a new language, one greatly enriched by the addition of Old French words.

Dined and *dinner,* which Lord Randal and his mother use in the second stanza of the ballad, are among the words derived from Old French. Some other words are *court, joy, beauty, dance, servant, heir, taste, story, government,* and *poet.*

Look up each of these words in a dictionary and note the Old French word from which it came. Words derived from French (one of the two major foreign sources of modern English; the other is Latin) are marked OF, MF, or F. Note that many of the words which entered the language from French came originally from Latin (L. or Lat.) or Greek (Gk.). If possible, note which of the words had the same meaning in French that they have in English.

Composition and Discussion

The following four stanzas appeared in later versions of "Lord Randal":

> "What d' ye leave to your mother, Lord Randal my son?
> What d' ye leave to your mother, my handsome
>   young man?"
> "Four and twenty milk kye,° mother, make my bed soon,
> For I'm sick at the heart, and I fain wald lie down."

5   "What d' ye leave to your sister, Lord Randal my son?
> What d' ye leave to your sister, my handsome
>   young man?"
> "My gold and my silver, mother, make my bed soon,
> For I'm sick at the heart, and I fain wald lie down."

> "What d' ye leave to your brother, Lord Randal
>   my son?
10 What d' ye leave to your brother, my handsome
>   young man?"
> "My houses and my lands, mother, make my bed soon,
> For I'm sick at the heart, and I fain wald lie down."

3. **kye:** cows.

"What d' ye leave to your true-love, Lord Randal
  my son?
What d' ye leave to your true-love, my handsome
  young man?"
15   "I leave her hell and fire, mother, make my bed soon,
For I'm sick at the heart, and I fain wald lie down."

    Discuss whether these four stanzas add to or detract from the
effect of the ballad. Why? Which version is more appealing? more
dramatic? Why?

Get Up and Bar the Door

It fell about the Martinmas time,
  And a gay time it was then,
When our goodwife° got puddings to make,
  And she's boiled them in the pan.

5   The wind so cold blew south and north,
  And blew into the floor;
Quoth our goodman° to our goodwife,
  "Go out and bar the door."

"My hand is in my hussyfskap,°
10   Goodman, as ye may see;
It should not be barred this hundred year,
  If it's to be barred by me!"

They made a paction° tween them two,
  They made it firm and sure,
15 That the first word whoe'er should speak,
  Should rise and bar the door.

Then by there came two gentlemen,
  At twelve o'clock at night,
And they could neither see house nor hall,
20   Nor coal nor candlelight.

3. goodwife: the equivalent of Mrs. **7. goodman:** the equivalent of
Mr. **9. hussyfskap:** housework. **13. paction:** agreement, pact.

"Now whether is this a rich man's house,
  Or whether is it a poor?"
But ne'er a word would one of them° speak
  For barring of the door.

25 And first they° ate the white puddings,
  And then they ate the black;
Though muckle° thought the goodwife to herself,
  Yet ne'er a word she spake.

Then said the one unto the other,
30 "Here, man, take ye my knife;
Do ye take off the old man's beard,
  And I'll kiss the goodwife."

"But there's no water° in the house,
  And what shall we do than?"
35 "What ails ye at the pudding broo,°
  That boils into° the pan?"

O up then started our goodman,
  An angry man was he:
"Will ye kiss my wife before my een,°
40 And scald me with pudding bree?"°

Then up and started our good wife,
  Gied° three skips on the floor:
"Goodman, you've spoken the foremost word,
  Get up and bar the door!"

23. them: the husband and the wife. **25. they:** the strangers.
27. muckle: much. **33. water:** probably to scald the beard and make
it easier to scrape off. **35. What . . . broo:** Why not use the pudding
broth? **36. into:** in. **39. een:** eyes. **40. bree:** broth, a hot liquid.
42. Gied: gave.

Meaning and Method

1. Although tragic events were the most frequent subjects of folk
ballads, humorous domestic situations, such as an argument
between a husband and wife, were also used. What was the

cause of the disagreement between husband and wife? What "paction" did they agree to? What does their behavior reveal about their characters? their relationship?

2. The details in lines 1–4 indicate that puddings were not usually part of the couple's meals. Why did the wife not protest when her puddings were being eaten? In your opinion, did the husband finally speak because he was less stubborn than the wife, or because he was threatened more directly? What does the wife's reaction to the husband's speech show about her character?

3. Why would this ballad *not* have been humorous if the men had stolen money or suggested that they would strangle the wife and cut the man's throat? What do eating puddings, kissing an old man's wife, and shaving a beard have in common? For example, are they events of great importance? Are they blown up out of proportion?

Language: Pronunciation and Spelling

Spelling does not always reflect present pronunciation, but it may reflect the original pronunciation of the word. For example, the word *knife* (spelled cnīf in Old English or Anglo-Saxon) was originally pronounced cə·nīf. The now silent first letter of such words as *gnaw, write,* and *knee* were also pronounced at one time. In these cases, spelling did not change to reflect changing pronunciation.

A contrasting peculiarity occurs with such words as *where, when,* and *what.* These were originally spelled hwær, hwæn, and hwat, respectively, and most English-speaking people still pronounce the /hw/ sounds of their original spelling.

In a dictionary, look up the words, *why, whether, whole, who,* and *white.* Which are pronounced with /hw/ sounds? Which are not? Why?

Composition

"Translate" this poem into modern English. For example, in line 30, you would write: "Here, man, you take my knife." Wherever possible, try to keep the original rhyme scheme and meter.

John Henry

This American Negro ballad tells the story of a heroic man who was both more and less powerful than the machine which was encroaching on his world.

When John Henry was a little fellow,
You could hold him in the palm of your hand,
He said to his pa, "When I grow up
I'm gonna be a steel-driving man,°
5   Gonna be a steel-driving man."

When John Henry was a little baby,
Setting on his mammy's knee,
He said, "The Big Bend Tunnel on the C. & O. Road°
Is gonna be the death of me,
10   Gonna be the death of me."

One day his captain told him,
How he had bet a man
That John Henry would beat his steam drill down,
Cause John Henry was the best in the land,
15   John Henry was the best in the land.

John Henry kissed his hammer,
White man turned on steam,
Shaker° held John Henry's trusty steel,
Was the biggest race the world had ever seen,
20   Lawd, biggest race the world ever seen.

John Henry on the right side,
The steam drill on the left,
"Before I'll let your steam drill beat me down,
I'll hammer my fool self to death,
25   Hammer my fool self to death."

4. steel-driving man: a man who hammered on the steel drill which, before the steam drill, was used to cut into rock. **8. C. & O. Road:** Chesapeake and Ohio railroad. **18. Shaker:** the man who held the steel drill.

Captain heard a mighty rumbling,
Said, "The mountain must be caving in,"
John Henry said to the captain,
"It's my hammer swinging in de wind,
30　　My hammer swinging in de wind."

John Henry said to his shaker,
"Shaker, you'd better pray;
For if ever I miss this piece of steel,
Tomorrow'll be your burial day,
35　　Tomorrow'll be your burial day."

John Henry said to his captain,
"Before I ever leave town,
Gimme a twelve-pound hammer wid a whale-bone
　　handle,
And I'll hammer dat steam drill on down,
40　　I'll hammer dat steam drill on down."

John Henry said to his captain,
"A man ain't nothin' but a man,
But before I'll let dat steam drill beat me down
I'll die wid my hammer in my hand,
45　　Die wid my hammer in my hand."

The man that invented the steam drill
He thought he was mighty fine,
John Henry drove down fourteen feet,
While the steam drill only made nine,
50　　Steam drill only made nine.

"Oh, lookaway over yonder, captain,
You can't see like me,"
He gave a long and loud and lonesome cry,
"Lawd, a hammer be the death of me,
55　　A hammer be the death of me!"

John Henry hammering on the mountain
As the whistle blew for half-past two,
The last words his captain heard him say,

"I've done hammered my insides in two,
60   Lawd, I've hammered my insides in two."

The hammer that John Henry swung
It weighed over twelve pound,
He broke a rib in his left hand side
And his intrels° fell on the ground,
65   And his intrels fell on the ground.

John Henry, O, John Henry,
His blood is running red,
Fell right down with his hammer to the ground
Said, "I beat him to the bottom but I'm dead,
70   Lawd, beat him to the bottom but I'm dead."

When John Henry was laying there dying,
The people all by his side,
The very last words they heard him say,
"Give me a cool drink of water 'fore I die,
75   Cool drink of water 'fore I die."

John Henry had a little woman,
The dress she wore was red,
She went down the track, and she never looked back,
Going where her man fell dead,
80   Going where her man fell dead.

They carried him down by the river,
And buried him in the sand,
And everybody that passed that way,
Said, "There lies that steel-driving man,
85   There lies a steel-driving man."

They carried him down by the river,
And buried him in the sand,
And every locomotive come a-roaring by,
Says, "There lies that steel-drivin' man,
90   Lawd, there lies a steel-drivin' man."

64. intrels: a dialectal pronunciation of *entrails.*

Some say he came from Georgia,
And some from Alabam,
But it's wrote on the rock at the Big Bend Tunnel,
That he was an East Virginia man,
95 Lawd, Lawd, an East Virginia man.

Meaning and Method

1. What characteristics of John Henry indicate that he was unlike ordinary men? Why is he, nevertheless, believable? What specific details contribute to the impression that John Henry is a real human being?
2. What was John Henry fighting for? That is, was his struggle against the captain? progress and modernity? his own stubborn pride? all these? In your opinion, did he win or lose? Do you admire, pity, or sympathize with him?
3. John Henry's comment, "A man ain't nothin' but a man" (line 42) is a theme of the ballad. What does it mean? Are there other themes in the ballad? If so, state them in your own words.
4. What physical action does the rhythm of this ballad imitate? Why is the rhythm appropriate for a work song—a song sung by workers at their jobs?

Composition

Although it was written approximately a century ago, "John Henry" is a song about the problem of automation—the use of machines to replace human labor. In a three- or four-paragraph composition, explain the benefits and disadvantages which result from automation. Use specific examples, real or imagined, to support your points.

SIR WALTER SCOTT
(1771–1832)

Like many of the writers of folk ballads, Sir Walter Scott lived for some time in the Border Country of Scotland. There he listened to the ballads of the Scottish past which he later collected in the three volumes of his *Minstrelsy of the Scottish Border.* The Border tales and ballads inspired him to write long narrative poems, one of which, *The Lay of the Last Minstrel,* made him famous when it was published in 1805.

Throughout his career, the land, people, and past of Scotland were Scott's primary interests. His best-known poem, *The Lady of the Lake,* illustrates his love for the Scottish countryside. The novels he wrote after his interest in poetry declined are, like his narrative poems, usually set in the heroic past of Scotland and are filled with action.

In his later years, Scott, like his fictional heroes, was forced to fight for his honor. His "adversary," however, was not a single person but the immense debts he had accumulated through unwise borrowing and the mismanagement of a publishing firm in which he had invested. He literally fought this battle with his pen, for he forced himself to turn out novel after novel in an effort to pay back his creditors. The creditors were finally repaid—but only after his death, when the copyrights to his novels were sold.

Proud Maisie *

Proud Maisie is in the wood,
    Walking so early;
Sweet Robin sits on the bush,
    Singing so rarely.

* **Proud Maisie:** a song sung by Madge Wildfire, a character in Scott's novel, *The Heart of Midlothian,* as she lay dying.

5   "Tell me, thou bonny bird,
          When shall I marry me?"—
       "When six braw° gentlemen
          Kirkward° shall carry ye."

       "Who makes the bridal bed,
10   Birdie, say truly?"—
       "The gray-headed sexton
          That delves° the grave duly.°

       "The glowworm o'er grave and stone
          Shall light thee steady.
15   The owl from the steeple sing,
          'Welcome, proud lady.'"

7. braw: fine.   **8. Kirkward:** churchward;   toward   the   church.
12. delves: digs;   **duly:** properly.

Meaning and Method

1. Maisie's character is suggested by her questions to the robin.
Does her first question reveal confidence? pride? a lighthearted
attitude? Maisie interprets the word *carry* in line 8 as meaning
"escort" instead of "bear" or "transport." What does her interpretation of the prophecy emphasize about her character?

2. What prophecy does the robin give? Why do you imagine
Scott chose a day bird, suggesting light and music, to give this
solemn warning? Why might he have chosen the *owl,* a night
bird, to sing from the steeple? Why a *glowworm* rather than a
candle to light Maisie's funeral? In your answers, consider the
connotations of each word.

3. At the beginning of the poem, a girl is walking in the woods
and a robin is singing: the reader expects to hear a pleasant tale.
At the end of the poem, however, the mood is somber. What
words in the poem help create first the light mood and then the
somber mood? How do the /s/ sounds in stanza one and the
/g/, /gr/, and /d/ sounds of lines 11–13 help emphasize the
two moods?

4. What is the main theme of "Proud Maisie"? How does the fact that this song is sung by a dying girl in Scott's novel emphasize the theme?

Composition

Write a composition in which you describe an imaginary encounter with a talking bird or animal, or a talking mechanical object such as a refrigerator, car, or computer. Include a detailed description of the setting as well as dialogue and action.

ROY HELTON
(born 1886)

Roy Helton would seem to have his roots in city culture, since he was born in Washington, D.C., and studied at the University of Pennsylvania in Philadelphia. However, his ancestors lived in the Appalachian hill country, and he has, as he says of himself, "wandered alone for the most part, over the Appalachians from Maine to Carolina, studying the people of the highlands from whom I came." His experiences in the Appalachians are reflected in many of his poems, which show the influence of the simple, direct manner of the mountain folk and the balladlike stories they still tell.

Old Christmas

This literary ballad is based on an old folk legend of the Kentucky hill people.

"Where you coming from, Lomey Carter,
  So airly° over the snow?
And what's them pretties° you got in your hand,
  And where you aiming to go?

5 "Step in, honey! Old Christmas° morning
  I ain't got nothing much;
Maybe a bite of sweetness and corn bread,
  A little ham meat and such.

2. airly: early. **3. pretties:** usually means toys or decorations. Here the word probably means cuttings from the elder bushes which are supposed to bloom in honor of the birth of Christ. **5. Old Christmas:** January 6th, the twelfth day of Christmas, is also known as Epiphany, Little Christmas, and Old Christmas. According to tradition, it was on this date that the Magi visited the infant Jesus. In some places, the birth of Jesus is also celebrated on this day, and gifts are exchanged.

"But come in, honey! Sally Anne Barton's
10   Hungering after your face.
Wait till I light my candle up:
          Set down! There's your old place.

"Now where you been so airly this morning?"
          "Graveyard, Sally Anne.
15   *Up by the trace° in the salt-lick° meadows*
Where Taulbe kilt my man."

"Taulbe ain't to home this morning. . . .
          I can't scratch up a light:
Dampness gets on the heads of the matches;
20   But I'll blow up the embers bright."

          "Needn't trouble. I won't be stopping:
          Going a long ways still."
"You didn't see nothing, Lomey Carter,
          Up on the graveyard hill?"

25   *"What should I see there, Sally Anne Barton?"*
          "Well, sperits do walk last night."
          "There were a elderbush° a-blooming
          While the moon still give some light."

"Yes, elderbushes, they bloom, Old Christmas,
30   And critters kneel down in their straw
Anything else up in the graveyard?"

          "One thing more I saw:
I saw my man with his head all bleeding
          Where Taulbe's shot went through."

35   "What did he say?"
                    "He stopped and kissed me."
          "What did he say to you?"

15. trace: path; **salt-lick:** a place in which there is a deposit of min-
eral salt which animals lick; therefore, good hunting ground.
27. elderbush: a shrub which usually blooms in the summer.

"Said, Lord Jesus forguv your Taulbe;
But he told me another word;
40   He said it soft when he stooped and kissed me.
That were the last I heard."

"Taulbe ain't home this morning."
"I know that, Sally Anne,
For I kilt him coming down through the meadow
45   Where Taulbe kilt my man.

"I met him upon the meadow trace
When the moon were fainting fast,
And I had my dead man's rifle gun
And kilt him as he came past."

50   "But I heard two shots."
"'Twas his was second:
He shot me 'fore he died:
You'll find us at daybreak, Sally Anne Barton:
I'm laying there dead at his side."

Meaning and Method

1. What details in the first stanzas of the ballad make you think
that Lomey and Sally Anne are or have been good friends?
What fact revealed later in the poem has affected their friendship?
2. How does Sally Anne know that "Taulbe ain't to home" (line
17)? Why does she repeat this statement in line 42? Does her
statement in line 50 that she had "heard two shots" indicate
that she might have been suspicious of Lomey at the beginning?
If so, why did she act in such a friendly way?
3. How has the poet created suspense in this ballad? What passages
in particular contribute to the overall suspense?
4. How does the fact that the murder takes place on Old Christmas emphasize the tragedy?
5. The poem includes some homey touches (e.g., Sally Anne in-
vites Lomey in for cornbread and ham) and uses the dialect of

Kentucky hill people. Note examples of each of these devices. Explain why you think they might have been used. What effect do they contribute? At what point in the poem does the reader discover that this is a ghost story?

Composition

Folk ballads have the following characteristics:

1. *Story told dramatically.* The listener may be plunged directly into the main action of the story, or suspense may be built up and the listener may not find out what has happened until the end of the ballad. Throughout the ballad, the listener or reader is shown things happening, rather than being told about them.

2. *Concentration on one major episode.* The events leading up to the crucial dramatic situation are not described in detail. All unnecessary information is omitted so that the listeners can concentrate on the narrator's, or storyteller's, account of the main action.

3. *Character types.* The characters are generally mothers and sons, husbands and wives, or lovers who do not have individual and unusual personalities. Character is sketched dramatically either through action or dialogue.

4. *Commonplace words and images.* Primarily denotative rather than connotative words are used because the listening audience does not have a chance to ponder each word. In the rare instances when a place or character is described, standard images, such as "milk-white hands," tend to be used.

5. *Repetition.* Important statements are repeated for emphasis. Often there is a refrain—a frequent repetition of the same line or lines.

6. *Impersonal narrator.* The narrator is primarily interested in telling a story. Although he often chooses to tell tales of people who are punished for something they have done, he rarely introduces his own judgments.

7. *Ballad stanzas.* Four-line stanzas, usually rhymed *abcb*, with four stressed syllables in the first and third lines and three stressed syllables in the second and fourth lines, are most commonly used (see page 100, question 3).

8. *Similar subject matter.* Current events, history, legends, love, and the supernatural are the most common subjects.

"Old Christmas" was written by a modern poet in imitation of folk ballads. Select one way in which "Old Christmas" is like a folk ballad, and, in a paragraph, give reasons to support your choice. In a second paragraph, give reasons why one characteristic in the list could *not* be applied to "Old Christmas."

RUDYARD KIPLING
(1865–1936)

Kipling was a child of both East and West. He was born of British parents in Bombay, India, when India was part of the British Empire. As a young boy, he spoke both English and Hindustani (the most widely used of the many languages spoken in India), and was taken by servants to Hindu as well as Christian religious services. From the ages of six to sixteen, he went to school in England, but returned to India to become a sub-editor of a small military newspaper and remained there for seven years.

His bicultural upbringing played a large part in the literary career that brought Kipling great popularity early in his life. It gave him a unique subject matter. British readers were eager to hear about the exotic world of India, and Kipling's narrators—generally soldiers or low-ranking government employees—provided a point of view with which most British people could identify.

Kipling's mastery of storytelling also contributed to his success. Both in prose and verse, he created vigorous, sympathetic characters and fast-paced narratives. Kipling had an excellent ear for speech patterns and could convey, with equal ease, the cockney dialect of a British soldier or the stilted English of an Indian, and make the dialogue flow naturally.

In 1907, these characteristics of his work were honored when he became the first Englishman to receive the Nobel Prize for literature. The peak of his popularity, however, had passed. The empire Kipling deeply admired was being reevaluated, and Kipling's feeling that it was the "white man's burden" to "civilize" the natives of non-Western countries, had become increasingly distasteful to many people. Despite its dated imperialistic views, much of his work has great vitality—the reader almost believes that British India still exists.

The Ballad of East and West

*Oh. East is East. and West is West, and never the twain shall
meet,*
*Till Earth and Sky stand presently at God's great Judgment
Seat;*
But there is neither East nor West, Border, nor Breed, nor Birth,
*When two strong men stand face to face, though they come
from the ends of the earth!*

5   Kamal° is out with twenty men to raise° the Border side,
And he has lifted° the Colonel's mare that is
    the Colonel's pride.
He has lifted her out of the stable-door between
    the dawn and the day,
And turned the calkins° upon her feet, and ridden her
    far away.
Then up and spoke the Colonel's son that led a troop
    of the Guides:°
10   "Is there never a man of all my men can say where
    Kamal hides?"
Then up and spoke Mohammed Khan, the son of the
    Ressaldar:°
"If ye know the track of the morning mist, ye know
    where his pickets° are.
At dusk he harries° the Abazai°—at dawn he is
    into Bonair,°
But he must go by Fort Bukloh to his own place
    to fare.
15   So if ye gallop to Fort Bukloh as fast as a bird can fly,

---

5. Kamal (kä·mal′): an Afghan chief who led raiding parties across
the border into northwest India; **raise:** stir up. **6. lifted:** stolen.
8. calkins (kôk′·inz): sharp-pointed metal pieces on horseshoes which
prevent slipping. **9. Guides:** native troops who served with the English. **11. Ressaldar:** a native commander of a troop of Indian cav-
alry. **12. pickets:** guards. **13. harries:** raids; **Abazai** (ə·bä·sē′),
Bonair (bun·âr′): settlements about forty miles apart on the northern
frontier of India.

By the favor of God ye may cut him off ere he win°
    to the Tongue of Jagai.°
But if he be past the Tongue of Jagai, right swiftly
    turn ye then,
For the length and the breadth of that grisly plain
    is sown with Kamal's men.
There is rock to the left, and rock to the right,
    and low lean thorn between,

20   And ye may hear a breech-bolt snick° where never
    a man is seen."
The Colonel's son has taken horse, and a raw rough dun°
    was he,
With the mouth of a bell and the heart of Hell
    and the head of a gallows-tree.°
The Colonel's son to the Fort has won, they bid him
    stay to eat—
Who rides at the tail of a Border thief, he sits not long
    at his meat.

25   He's up and away from Fort Bukloh as fast as he can fly,
Till he was aware of his father's mare in the gut°
    of the Tongue of Jagai,
Till he was aware of his father's mare with Kamal upon
    her back,
And when he could spy the white of her eye, he made
    the pistol crack.
He has fired once, he has fired twice, but the whistling
    ball went wide.

30   "Ye shoot like a soldier," Kamal said. "Show now if ye
    can ride!"
It's up and over the Tongue of Jagai, as blown
    dust-devils° go;
The dun he fled like a stag of ten, but the mare like
    a barren doe.

---

16. win: succeed in reaching; **Tongue of Jagai:** a pass between the
hills. **20. breech-bolt snick:** the sound of a rifle being loaded and
cocked. **21. dun:** a horse of nearly neutral, slightly brownish dark
gray. **22. gallows-tree:** a wooden construction used for hanging a
person it has two upright beams and a crossbeam. **26. gut:** a narrow
passageway (as a strait or a gulley.) **31. dust-devils:** small whirl-
winds that lift dust or sand often to great heights, which seem to change
shape as they move along.

The dun he leaned against the bit and slugged
   his head above,
But the red mare played with the snaffle-bars,° as
   a maiden plays with a glove.
35 There was rock to the left and rock to the right, and
   low, lean thorn between;
And thrice he heard a breech-bolt snick tho' never
   a man was seen.
They had ridden the low moon out of the sky,
   their hoofs drum up the dawn.
The dun he went like a wounded bull, but the mare like
   a new-roused fawn.
The dun he fell at a watercourse°—in a woeful heap
   fell he;
40 And Kamal has turned the red mare back, and
   pulled the rider free.
He has knocked the pistol out of his hand—small room
   was there to strive.
"'Twas only by favor of mine," quoth he, "ye rode
   so long alive:
There was not a rock for twenty mile, there was not
   a clump of tree,
But covered a man of my own men with his rifle cocked
   on his knee.
45 If I had raised my bridle-hand, as I have held it low,
The little jackals° that flee so fast were feasting all
   in a row:
If I had bowed my head on my breast, as I have held it
   high,
The kite° that whistles above us now were gorged till
   she could not fly."
Lightly answered the Colonel's son: "Do good to bird
   and beast,
50 But count who come for the broken meats before
   thou makest a feast.
If there should follow a thousand swords to carry
   my bones away,

34. snaffle-bars: bridle bit. **39. watercourse:** a stream, river, or
brook. **46. jackals:** doglike animals that feed on small animals and
dead flesh. **48. kite:** a bird that feeds on dead flesh; a member of the
hawk family.

Belike° the price of a jackal's meal were more than
a thief could pay.
They° will feed their horse on the standing crop,
their men on the garnered° grain,
The thatch of the byres° will serve their fires when all
the cattle are slain.
55 But if thou thinkest the price be fair,—thy brethren wait
to sup,
The hound is kin to the jackal-spawn,°—howl, dog,
and call them up!
And if thou thinkest the price be high, in steer° and gear
and stack,°
Give me my father's mare again, and I'll fight my own
way back!"
Kamal has gripped him by the hand and set him upon
his feet.
60 "No talk shall be of dogs," said he, "when wolf and
gray wolf meet.
May I eat dirt if thou hast hurt of° me in deed or breath;
What dam° of lances brought thee forth to jest
at the dawn with Death?"
Lightly answered the Colonel's son: "I hold by the blood
of my clan:
Take up the mare for my father's gift—by God, she has
carried a man!"
65 The red mare ran to the Colonel's son and nuzzled
against his breast;
"We be two strong men," said Kamal then, "but she
loveth the younger best.
So she shall go with a lifter's dower,° my turquoise-
studded rein,
My 'broidered saddle and saddlecloth, and silver
stirrups twain."
The Colonel's son a pistol drew, and held it muzzle end,
70 "Ye have taken the one from a foe," said he; "Will ye
take the mate from a friend?"

---

52. Belike: perhaps. **53. They:** the British soldiers; **garnered:**
gathered. **54. byres:** barns. **56. spawn:** offspring. **57. steer:**
steers; **stack:** grain. **61. hurt   of:** been   hurt   by. **62. dam:**
mother. **67. lifter's dower:** dowry, or gift, given by a thief.

"A gift for a gift," said Kamal straight; "a limb
  for the risk of a limb.
Thy father has sent his son to me, I'll send my son
  to him!"
With that he whistled his only son, that dropped from
  a mountain crest—
He trod the ling° like a buck in spring, and he looked
  like a lance in rest.
75   "Now here is thy master," Kamal said, "who leads
  a troop of the Guides,
And thou must ride at his left side as shield on shoulder
  rides.
Till Death or I cut loose the tie, at camp and board
  and bed,
Thy life is his—thy fate it is to guard him with thy head.
So, thou must eat the White Queen's° meat, and all
  her foes are thine,
80   And thou must harry thy father's hold° for the peace
  of the Border-line.
And thou must make a trooper tough and hack thy way
  to power—
Belike they will raise thee to Ressaldar when I am
  hanged in Peshawur!"°

They have looked each other between the eyes, and
  there have found no fault.
They have taken the Oath of the Brother-in-Blood
  on leavened bread° and salt;°
85   They have taken the Oath of the Brother-in-Blood
  on fire and fresh-cut sod,°
On the hilt and the haft of the Khyber knife,° and
  the Wondrous Names of God.°

---

74. ling: heather, a shrub. **79. White Queen:** Queen Victoria of
England, who was also Empress of India. **80. hold:** stronghold.
82. Peshawur (pə·shä′wər): the center of the British government in
Northwest Frontier Province. **84. leavened bread:** When yeast is
added to dough, the dough rises. The risen dough when baked is called
leavened bread; **salt:** a traditional sign of friendship. **85. sod:** soil
which is held together by matted grass roots; sometimes used to make
fires. **86. Khyber** (kĭ′bər) **knife:** named for the Khyber Pass, a narrow pass between India and Afghanistan; **Wondrous Names of God:**
one hundred Moslem names given to God.

The Colonel's son he rides the mare and Kamal's boy
the dun,
And two have come back to Fort Bukloh where there
went forth but one.
And when they drew to the Quarter-Guard,° full
twenty swords flew clear—
90   There was not a man but carried his feud with the blood
of the mountaineer.
"Ha' done! ha' done!" said the Colonel's son. "Put up
the steel at your sides!
Last night ye had struck at a Border thief—tonight 'tis
a man of the Guides!"

*Oh, East is East, and West is West, and never the twain
shall meet,*
*Till Earth and Sky stand presently at God's great Judgment
Seat;*
95   *But there is neither East nor West, Border, nor Breed, nor
Birth,*
*When two strong men stand face to face, though they come
from the ends of the earth!*

89. Quarter-Guard: sentries.

Meaning and Method

1. Why was Kamal being pursued? What does Mohammed Khan
tell the Colonel's son about Kamal?
2. Why did Kamal challenge the Colonel's son to a race? Why did
he pull the rider free after the dun had fallen down? Why did
he not kill the Colonel's son? Explain what you learn about
Kamal's character from the answers to these questions. Do you
think that Kamal is an ordinary thief? Why does he steal?
3. Explain in your own words the speech of the Colonel's son in
lines 49–58. What does this speech show about his character?
Does he frighten Kamal with his threats?
4. What do the two men admire about each other? In your answer, explain Kamal's words in lines 60–62 and line 66, and
those of the Colonel's son in lines 63–64.

5. What physical action does the rhythm of the poem suggest? Why is the rhythmic effect appropriate?

6. The first and last stanzas state the main theme of the poem. What is it? How does the story of Kamal and the Colonel's son illustrate this theme?

7. In line 62, Kamal asks the Colonel's son: "What dam of lances brought thee forth to jest at the dawn with Death?" In this question, he is obviously considering Death as a person, someone with whom the Colonel's son could jest. He is therefore using *personification,* a figure of speech in which human qualities are attributed to an animal, object, or idea. Kamal's "Death" is a personified idea.

In line 77, Kamal makes another reference to Death. Is this reference also an example of personification? Explain.

STEPHEN VINCENT BENÉT*
(1898–1943)

All of America was home to Stephen Vincent Benét. He was born in Bethlehem, Pennsylvania, but because his father was an army officer, he lived in California, Kentucky, and Georgia. He attended Yale University in Connecticut, and was later married in Chicago. After brief European travels, he lived in Rhode Island and finally settled in New York City.

Benét's love for his country and its various regions is evident in his poetry, much of which is about America. His imaginative portraits of the American present and past, particularly that of *John Brown's Body,* a verse narrative which won the Pulitzer Prize for poetry in 1929, gained him enormous popularity.

Benét's choice of the abolitionist John Brown was characteristic, for in both his fiction and poetry, he showed a strong interest in extraordinary historical characters. His short story, "The Devil and Daniel Webster," which was made into a play, an opera, and a movie, presents the famous American orator as being so clever that he beats the devil in a verbal duel. His narrative poem "The Ballad of Marco Polo" tells a true but almost unbelievable adventure story about three Venetian traders who visited the fabulous land of Cathay (China) two centuries before Columbus' voyage to America. In both of these works, and in others, he shows that he is a master of dramatic technique, as he draws the reader along with him to the border between fantasy and reality.

* **Benét** (bə·nā′).

The Ballad of Marco Polo

Marco Polo, curious man,
What drove you to seek for Kublai Khan? °

Perhaps it was youth, for I was young,
Perhaps it was my father's tongue
5   The desert hawk I had never seen
Till the years of my age were turned fifteen,
For I was not born when he went away
To trade beyond the rim of the day, °
And, when he returned, we were strange and shy,
10 Meeting each other, he and I,
For a lost bride's eyes looked out at him,
My mother's, who died in bearing me,
And the lines in his visage° were great and grim
And I knew he had been in Tartary. °

15 *Marco Polo, how did it fall*
That at last you followed him, after all?

When the world shut in with candlelight,
They° would talk to each other, night on night,
While the water lapped at the landing stair °
20 And they hardly knew that I was there
Except as a shadow the candle threw
When the wind before the morning blew
And the great house creaked like a ship of stone,
Maffeo and Nicolo,
25 Talking of marvels past renown,

2. Kublai Khan (ko͞o′blī kän′): thirteenth-century ruler of China and great-grandson of Genghis Khan. The Khans, who came from Mongolia, north of China proper, conquered China. The word *khan* means lord or prince. **7–8. he went . . . day:** His father Nicolo and his uncle Maffeo Polo left in 1260, two years after the trade routes to China had been opened for the first time. **13. visage** (viz′ij): face or facial expression. **14. Tartary:** a region of Asia under Mongol leadership in the thirteenth and fourteenth centuries. The people of Tartary were called Tartars. **18. They:** Marco's father and uncle. **19. While . . . stair:** Because the city has a series of interlocking canals, many Venetian houses have landings with stairs where boats dock.

Talking of wonders still to do—
Their talk was honey and wine and snow,
How could I help but drink it down?
How could I help but thirst and burn,
30   When they opened the bag of camel's hair
And looked at the marvel hidden there
And said, "It is time and we must return"?

Marco Polo, what did you see,
When at length you came to Tartary?

35   I know I have been where I have been,
But how can I tell you what I have seen?
I know the desert of the dry tree
Whose branches bear eternity,
And the hot sickness of the noon.
40   I drank the mare's milk of the tents,
I saw the musk ox gape at me,
I have had gold and frankincense°
And silks that glitter like the moon,
But what can I tell that will make you see?

45   *Marco Polo, wandering sword,*
What manner of man did you call lord?

I have been the pope's and the doge's° man,
But I never knew master like Kublai Khan.
The sons of his body sit ten by ten
50   At buffets of precious napery,°
When he hunts, he hunts with ten thousand men
And his Tartar falcons darken the sky,
He has jewels uncounted and golden plate
Whence even his meanest slaves may eat,
55   And he sits and numbers the hairs of fate
With a great, tame lion crouched at his feet,
And his mercy as fair as a white ram's fleece,

42. frankincense: a fragrant substance made from Arabian or East African herbs. **47. doge** (dōzh): the chief magistrate of the city of Venice when it was an independent republic. **50. buffets** (boo͞·făz′) . . . **napery** (nā′pər·ē): *here,* tables set with precious table linen.

Mighty in battle and just in peace,
Star of the city of Kanbalu,°
60   Khan of Khans° and Great of the Great
Whose bounty falls like the morning dew—
Since Adam delved° and Eve span°
Who ever saw prince like Kublai Khan?

Marco Polo, tell me how
65   *Your Venice° talks of your travels now.*

They call me braggart, they call me liar,
They gawk at me like an eater of fire,
"Millions" Polo, the fable-monger,
Who dines on a lizard to stay his hunger,
70   Such being his custom in Cathay.
But they laughed with their beards another way,
When we came back in '95°
Like ghosts returned to a world alive,
With our gear still smelling of musk and civet°
75   And my father's beard grown whiter than privet,°
Two old men and a younger one
Who had looked in the eye of the Eastern sun
And lived—and lived to tell the tale
Which I tell to the shadows in this, my jail.
80   Why, my very cousins did not own° us
And the jeering crowd was ready to stone us
Till we ripped the riches out of our rags
And proved we were Polos—by moneybags!

Let them laugh as long as they like today!
85   I have seen Cathay, I have seen Cathay!
Their little Europe—their dwarfish West—

59. Kanbalu: the capital of China; now Peking.   **60. Khan of Khans:** Prince of Princes.   **62. delved:** dug;   **span:** old past tense of spin.   **65. Venice** (ven'əs): At this time, Venice was the greatest European trading city. However, her ships did not venture past the bounds of Europe and Africa.   **72. '95:** 1295. Marco Polo stayed in Cathay for nineteen years.   **74. musk and civet:** substances used in making perfume.   **75. privet:** a bushy shrub with white flowers and black berries.   **80. own:** *here,* admit they knew.

Their doge with his ring and his marriage fee!°
I have stolen the eggs from the phoenix° nest
And walked by the shores of the Ocean-Sea,°
90   The earth-encircler, the Asian main,

And, if Kublai lived, I would go again,
For what is their quarrel of gimcrack° lords,
Their toy fleets sailing a herring pond,
By the might that mastered the Tartar hordes?
95   There are worlds beyond, there are worlds beyond,
Worlds to be conquered, worlds to be found
By the river and desert and burning ground,
Even, perchance, by the Ocean-Sea
If a man has courage enough to dare,
100   And I know that others will follow me
And I mark the roads that will take them there,
The roads of the golden caravan,
The whole great East in its roaring youth,
For—there was a prince named Kublai Khan—
105   And I, the liar, have told the truth.

87. marriage fee: the doge collected a fee for licensing marriages.
88. phoenix (fē′niks): a legendary bird; it is supposed to be consumed
by its own fire, and then rise young from the ashes. **89. Ocean-Sea:** a
great ocean was believed to surround Europe, Asia, and Africa. No one
dreamed of the existence of America on the other side of the ocean.
92. gimcrack (jim′krak): showy but cheap.

Meaning and Method

1. Why do the people of Venice not believe Marco's tales? What
   made them believe the Polos in '95? What do these reactions
   show about human nature?
2. Why does Marco himself not believe that he can make people
   see what he has seen? What examples does he give to show how
   exotic and luxurious Kublai Khan's domain is? What words or
   phrases make Europe seem small, poor, and confined by comparison?

3. Review the meaning of simile and metaphor. Read each of the following figures of speech and tell what ideas each compresses into a few concrete words.
   a. "beyond the rim of the day" (line 8)
   b. "the great house creaked like a ship of stone" (line 23)
   c. "Their talk was honey and wine and snow" (line 27)
   d. "his mercy as fair as a white ram's fleece" (line 57)
4. What sets Marco Polo apart from the Venetians? Why does he not care if they laugh? What has he gained from his adventure? Why did he go? State the theme of the poem, commenting particularly on lines 95–105.
5. The narrative, unlike those in the other poems you have read, is told by a speaker talking in the first person, as *I*. How does this *I* point of view add to the effect of the poem?

Language: Words Derived from Mythology

Marco Polo in Benét's poem says that Kublai Khan "sits and numbers the hairs of fate" (line 55). In his view, Kublai Khan is so powerful that he controls fate, or the forces which govern our future.

The word *fate* is derived from a story in Greek mythology. (*Mythology* is a collection of the fables or tales of a particular people. Usually these tales describe the exploits of gods and heroes, and attempt to provide explanations for life as it is. Each of these tales is called a *myth*.) The Fates were supposed to have been three sisters. The first one spun the thread of life, the second one measured the thread, and the third one snipped it off. No plans made by people had any effect on the Fates.

Many other words have been derived from the myths of the ancient Greeks and Romans. Among these words are the following:

1. fortune	5. muse
2. atlas	6. martial
3. titanic	7. phosphorus
4. sphinx	8. helium

Look up these words in a dictionary. Explain in class the meaning and origin of each of these words.

Composition

1. In Marco Polo's day, not much of the earth was known to Europeans, and the possibilities for exploration were enormous. Today, with most of the earth's surface mapped, written about, and photographed, adventurers turn to the sea and outer space.

Write a short composition in which you explain why you would like to explore the moon, another planet, or another galaxy. Either try to communicate your feelings about the trip, or discuss what you expect to find. Your composition may be humorous or serious.

2. Although the great explorations of the earth have been made, every person can explore part of the earth for himself or herself. Write a short composition about a large or small exploration in which you took part or would like to take part. For example, you might have explored a campsite, a river or lake, a beach, an attic or cellar, a new neighborhood, etc. Describe what you found and tell how you reacted to your "discoveries." Try to tell the story of your "exploration" in such a way that your "discoveries" are presented in chronological order.

ROBERT FROST

A biographical sketch of Robert Frost appears on page 60.

Two Tramps in Mud Time

Out of the mud two strangers came
And caught me splitting wood in the yard,
And one of them put me off my aim
By hailing cheerily "Hit them hard!"
5   I knew pretty well why he dropped behind
And let the other go on a way.
I knew pretty well what he had in mind:
He wanted to take my job for pay.

Good blocks of beech it was I split,
10   As large around as the chopping block;
And every piece I squarely hit
Fell splinterless as a cloven° rock.
The blows that a life of self-control
Spares to strike° for the common good
15   That day, giving a loose to my soul,
I spent on the unimportant wood.

The sun was warm but the wind was chill.
You know how it is with an April day
When the sun is out and the wind is still,
20   You're one month on in the middle of May.
But if you so much as dare to speak,
A cloud comes over the sunlit arch,
A wind comes off a frozen peak,
And you're two months back in the middle of March.

25   A bluebird comes tenderly up to alight
And fronts the wind to unruffle a plume,
His song so pitched as not to excite
A single flower as yet to bloom.

12. cloven: parted; split. **14. Spares to strike:** refrains from striking.

It is snowing a flake: and he half knew
30 Winter was only playing possum.
Except in color he isn't blue,
But he wouldn't advise a thing to blossom.

The water for which we may have to look
In summertime with a witching wand,°
35 In every wheelrut's now a brook,
In every print of a hoof a pond.
Be glad of water, but don't forget
The lurking frost in the earth beneath
That will steal forth after the sun is set
40 And show on the water its crystal teeth.

The time when most I loved my task
These two must make me love it more
By coming with what they came to ask.
You'd think I never had felt before
45 The weight of an ax-head poised aloft,
The grip on earth of outspread feet.
The life of muscles rocking soft
And smooth and moist in vernal° heat.

Out of the woods two hulking tramps
50 (From sleeping God knows where last night,
But not long since in the lumber camps).
They thought all chopping was theirs of right.
Men of the woods and lumberjacks,
They judged me by their appropriate tool.
55 Except as a fellow handled an ax,
They had no way of knowing a fool.

Nothing on either side was said.
They knew they had but to stay their stay
And all their logic would fill my head:
60 As that I had no right to play
With what was another man's work for gain.
My right might be love but theirs was need.

34. **witching wand:** a twig which some believe will lead the holder to
water.   48. **vernal:** spring (*ver* is the Latin word for spring).

And where the two exist in twain
Theirs was the better right—agreed.

65 But yield who will to their separation,
My object in living is to unite
My avocation and my vocation°
As my two eyes make one in sight.
Only where love and need are one,
70 And the work is play for mortal stakes,
Is the deed ever really done
For Heaven and the future's sakes.

67. avocation . . . vocation: A vocation is an occupation, something
for which you are paid; an avocation is a hobby—work for its own sake
or reward. (The prefix *a-* means "not" or "without.")

Meaning and Method

1. The speaker is displeased to see the strangers because he knows
they want to chop the wood to earn money. What words or
phrases in the second stanza show that the speaker fulfills a
personal need by chopping the wood himself? What indicates
that the act helps him release tension and a desire to do violent
acts? Why is the wood called "unimportant" (line 16)?
2. In stanzas three through five, the speaker describes the delicate
balance between spring and winter weather. In lines 19–24,
how does he show that this balance is impermanent? Point out
where he contrasts the abundance of water in spring with the
lack in summer. How does the warning of lines 37–40 show
that winter's danger underlies the hint of spring?
3. Referring to lines 44–48, explain what the speaker loves about
the job. How does he indicate the balance required for the act?
4. Does the speaker agree partly, entirely, or not at all that the
tramps' need is a "better right" (line 64)? that "all chopping" is
"theirs of right" (line 52)? His attempt to resolve this question
of right leads the speaker to state his "object in living" (line 66).
What is it? Does he try to balance or unite opposites in his life?
Does chopping the wood fulfill his objective at the moment?
5. In your own words, tell the story of this poem, stating its conflict. Do we know how the conflict is resolved? That is, do we
know whether the speaker keeps on chopping or lets the tramps
take over?

Language: Prefixes

Words are often formed to indicate that they are the opposite of something else. For example, *avocation* is the opposite of *vocation;* *unfriendly* is the opposite of *friendly; nonsense* is the opposite of *sense; impossible* is the opposite of *possible;* and *dislike* is the opposite of *like.* In these cases, the prefixes, or fixed forms at the beginning of the words (*a-, un-, non-, im-,* and *dis-*) all have negative meanings.

Prefixes, however, are not always negative. For example, the prefix *re-* means "back" or "again." The word *return* therefore means "to turn back"; the word *resell* means "to sell again."

Other common prefixes which do not have negative meanings are *pre-, post-, en-, ex-,* and *com-.*

Look up the meanings of these prefixes in a dictionary. Then find several words starting with each of these prefixes whose meanings reflect that of the prefix.

EDGAR ALLAN POE
(1809–1849)

Poe lived a life as dark and twisted as the plots of many of his short stories and poems. After the desertion of his alcoholic father and the death of his mother when Poe was only two, he became the ward of a wealthy, childless couple. The Allans educated him well, but Poe never felt loved by them. He quarreled more and more seriously with his foster father as he grew older. Conflicts arising out of Poe's undisciplined career as a student at the University of Virginia and as an appointee to West Point resulted in a complete break with John Allan.

The break freed him to pursue his ambitions as a writer, but it did not free him of troubles. By 1829 he had published two volumes of poetry and by 1835 became the editor of *The Southern Literary Messenger*. However, the career of the brilliant, erratic Poe was interrupted by the constant need for money. Also, his adored wife Virginia (a cousin half his age) developed tuberculosis in 1842 and died in only five years. After this blow, Poe became increasingly unstable. In 1849 he was found dead outside a tavern in Baltimore, and his body was placed in a nameless grave.

Poe's life is reflected in his poems and short stories, whose characters are often haunted literally or figuratively by the dark forces of life. Many of his most famous stories are horror stories or sinister detective stories, a form of which he is considered the inventor. Some of his poems, particularly "The Raven" and "The Haunted Palace," also illustrate this morbidity.

In other poems, however, notably "Annabel Lee," he often imagines an incandescently bright world of love, in which a gloomy, tortured man worships a glorious woman who is out of his reach—usually because she is dead. At his most optimistic, Poe imagines the ecstatic world of his dreams being realized after death.

The moods of ecstasy and horror—the twin poles which so intensely attracted Poe—are communicated to the reader partly through dazzling technical effects, for Poe used all manner of virtuoso sound devices to achieve a single effect. Critical judgment of the results varies. Many agree with James Russell Lowell, who in his *Fable for Critics* wrote:

There comes Poe with his raven, like Barnaby Rudge,*
Three-fifths sheer genius, and two-fifths sheer fudge.

Others echo the inscription on the bronze and marble memorial set up for him in the New York Museum of Art in 1855: He was great in his genius, unhappy in his life, wretched in his death. But in his fame he is immortal.

* **Barnaby Rudge:** the hero of Dickens' novel of the same name; he was a half-witted youth who was always accompanied by a raven.

The Raven

Once upon a midnight dreary, while I pondered,
    weak and weary,
Over many a quaint and curious volume of forgotten
    lore—
While I nodded, nearly napping, suddenly there came
    a tapping,
As of someone gently rapping, rapping at my chamber
    door.
5   "'Tis some visitor," I muttered, "tapping at my chamber
    door—
        Only this, and nothing more."

Ah, distinctly I remember it was in the bleak December,
And each separate dying ember wrought its ghost
    upon the floor.
Eagerly I wished the morrow;—vainly I had sought
    to borrow
10   From my books surcease° of sorrow—sorrow for the lost
    Lenore—
For the rare and radiant maiden whom the angels named
    Lenore—
        Nameless *here* for evermore.

10. surcease: end.

And the silken, sad, uncertain rustling of each purple
    curtain
Thrilled me—filled me with fantastic terrors never felt
    before;
15   So that now, to still the beating of my heart,
    I stood repeating,
"'Tis some visitor entreating entrance at my chamber
    door—
Some late visitor entreating entrance at my chamber
    door;—
        This it is and nothing more."

Presently my soul grew stronger; hesitating then
    no longer,
20   "Sir," said I, "or Madam, truly your forgiveness
    I implore;
But the fact is I was napping, and so gently you came
    rapping,
And so faintly you came tapping, tapping at my chamber
    door,
That I scarce was sure I heard you"—here I opened wide
    the door:
        Darkness there and nothing more.

25   Deep into that darkness peering, long I stood there
    wondering, fearing,
Doubting, dreaming dreams no mortal ever dared
    to dream before;
But the silence was unbroken, and the stillness gave
    no token,
And the only word there spoken was the whispered word,
  "Lenore?"
This I whispered, and an echo murmured back the word,
  "Lenore!"
30   Merely this, and nothing more.

Back into the chamber turning, all my soul within me
    burning,
Soon again I heard a tapping somewhat louder
    than before.

"Surely," said I, "surely that is something at my window
 lattice;
Let me see, then, what thereat is, and this mystery
 explore—
Let my heart be still a moment and this mystery
 explore;—
                'Tis the wind, and nothing more!"

Open here I flung the shutter, when, with many a flirt
 and flutter,
In there stepped a stately Raven of the saintly days
 of yore;°
Not the least obeisance° made he; not a minute
 stopped or stayed he;
But, with mien° of lord or lady, perched above my
 chamber door—
Perched upon a bust of Pallas° just above my chamber
 door—
                Perched, and sat, and nothing more.

Then this ebony bird beguiling my sad fancy into smiling,
By the grave and stern decorum of the countenance
 it wore,
"Though thy crest be shorn and shaven, thou," I said,
 "art sure no craven,
Ghastly, grim, and ancient Raven, wandering from
 the Nightly shore—
Tell me what thy lordly name is on the Night's Plutonian°
 shore!"
                Quoth the Raven, "Nevermore."

Much I marvelled this ungainly fowl to hear discourse
 so plainly,
Though its answer little meaning—little relevancy bore;
For we cannot help agreeing that no living human being

35

40

45

50

---

38. yore: long ago. **39. obeisance** (ō·bā′səns): act of expressing
respect. **40. mien** (mēn): air or manner. **41. Pallas** (pal′əs): Pallas
Athene, Greek goddess of wisdom. **47. Plutonian** (plōō·tō′nē·ən):
hellish; in Greek and Roman mythology, Pluto presided over the regions of the dead.

Ever yet was blessed with seeing bird above his chamber
    door—
Bird or beast upon the sculptured bust above his chamber
    door,
             With such name as "Nevermore."

55   But the Raven, sitting lonely on the placid bust,
        spoke only
That one word, as if his soul in that one word he did
    outpour.
Nothing farther then he uttered—not a feather then
    he fluttered—
Till I scarcely more than muttered, "Other friends
    have flown before—
On the morrow *he* will leave me, as my Hopes have
    flown before."
60   Then the bird said, "Nevermore."

Startled at the stillness broken by reply so aptly spoken,
"Doubtless," said I, "what it utters is its only stock
    and store
Caught from some unhappy master whom unmerciful
    Disaster
Followed fast and followed faster till his songs one burden
    bore—
65   Till the dirges° of his Hope that melancholy burden bore
             Of "Never—nevermore."

But the Raven still beguiling all my fancy into smiling,
Straight I wheeled a cushioned seat in front of bird
    and bust and door;
Then, upon the velvet sinking, I betook myself to linking
70   Fancy unto fancy, thinking what this ominous bird
    of yore—
What this grim, ungainly, ghastly, gaunt, and ominous
    bird of yore
             Meant in croaking "Nevermore."

65. dirges: funeral songs.

This I sat engaged in guessing, but no syllable expressing
To the fowl whose fiery eyes now burned into my
    bosom's core;
75   This and more I sat divining,° with my head at ease
    reclining
On the cushion's velvet lining that the lamplight
    gloated o'er,
But whose velvet-violet lining with the lamplight
    gloating o'er,
            She shall press, ah, nevermore!

Then, methought, the air grew denser, perfumed
    from an unseen censer°
80   Swung by seraphim° whose footfalls tinkled
    on the tufted floor.
"Wretch," I cried, "thy God hath lent thee—by these
    angels he hath sent thee
Respite—respite and nepenthe° from thy memories
    of Lenore;
Quaff,° oh, quaff this kind nepenthe and forget this lost
    Lenore!"
            Quoth the Raven, "Nevermore."

85   "Prophet!" said I, "thing of evil—prophet still, if bird
    or devil!
Whether Tempter sent, or whether tempest tossed thee
    here ashore,
Desolate, yet all undaunted, on this desert land
    enchanted—
On this home by Horror haunted—tell me truly,
    I implore—
Is there—*is* there balm in Gilead?°—tell me—tell me,
    I implore!"
90   Quoth the Raven, "Nevermore."

---

75. divining: conjecturing or surmising about a future event by insight or instinct. **79. censer:** *here,* a vessel which contains burning incense. **80. seraphim** (ser'ə·fim): the highest order of angels. **82. nepenthe** (ni·pen'thē): a drug that brings forgetfulness or makes suffering more bearable. **83. Quaff:** drink deeply. **89. balm in Gilead** (gil'ē·ad): Gilead in ancient Palestine produced a healing ointment. The expression, which means "relief from affliction," was used by the prophet Jeremiah. (See Jeremiah 8:22 and 46:11.)

"Prophet!" said I, "thing of evil—prophet still, if bird
   or devil!
By that Heaven that bends above us—by that God
   we both adore—
Tell this soul with sorrow laden if, within the distant
   Aidenn,°
It shall clasp a sainted maiden whom the angels name
   Lenore—
95 Clasp a rare and radiant maiden whom the angels name
   Lenore."
            Quoth the Raven, "Nevermore."

"Be that word our sign of parting, bird or fiend!"
   I shrieked, upstarting—
"Get thee back into the tempest and the Night's
   Plutonian shore!
Leave no black plume as a token of that lie thy soul hath
   spoken!
100 Leave my loneliness unbroken!—quit the bust above my
   door!
Take thy beak from out my heart, and take thy form
   from off my door!"
            Quoth the Raven, "Nevermore."

And the Raven, never flitting, still is sitting, *still* is sitting
On the pallid bust of Pallas just above my chamber door;
105 And his eyes have all the seeming of a demon's that is
   dreaming,
And the lamplight o'er him streaming throws his shadow
   on the floor;
And my soul from out that shadow that lies floating
   on the floor
            Shall be lifted—nevermore!

93. Aidenn (ā′dən): Arabic for Eden.

Meaning and Method

1. Point out words and reactions of the speaker that reveal his state
of mind at the beginning of the poem. What details of the room

and its furnishings contribute to a mood or atmosphere of gloom?

2. Why is Lenore important to the speaker? Does he want to remember or forget her? Does he have any hope that they will be reunited?

3. How and why does the speaker's attitude toward the raven change? Does he take it seriously at first? What does he come to believe the raven can tell him? How is hope shattered for the speaker in lines 79–84 and 92–96? What does he mean when he says that his soul will never be lifted "from out that shadow that lies floating on the floor"?

4. What do the repetition of the word *nevermore* and the choice of the word *raven* add to the effect of the poem? Could the words *no* and *blackbird* be substituted as effectively?

5. Poe is famous for his use of complicated rhyme patterns. In this poem, for example, all of the end rhymes end with the sound /or/. The effect is similar to that of a man frequently hitting one note on a piano; it emphasizes the speaker's obsession with Lenore. Is there a pattern in his use of internal rhymes? If so, what is it?

Language: Allusions to Mythology

Myths (see page 133), like ballads and legends, are the products of folk culture, and tell of the supposed deeds of gods and goddesses or heroes and heroines. The stories are not true, but they may reveal truths if they are understood symbolically.

The most famous myths in the West are those of the Greeks and the Romans. When the Romans conquered Greece, they adopted the Greek deities or gods, but usually changed their names. For example, the Greek goddess Pallas Athene (or Athena), alluded to in line 41, was called Minerva by the Romans. Allusions to Greek and Roman mythology appear frequently in Western literature.

The Greek and Roman deities were personifications of human and natural forces and activities. There were, among others, gods of love, war, the sun, the moon, the sea, earth, and death. Each god or goddess was thought to rule over one or more spheres of activity, and each had a symbol or symbols identified with him or her. The symbol of Jupiter or Jove (Roman) or Zeus (Greek), king of the gods, was a thunderbolt; the symbol of Athene or Minerva, goddess of wisdom, was the owl.

Check a dictionary or a book of mythology and identify the following gods and goddesses as to their functions and, if possible, the objects with which they were associated.

Greek	Roman
Hera	Juno
Aphrodite	Venus
Ares	Mars
Pluto (Hades)	Pluto (Dis)
Poseidon	Neptune
Apollo	Apollo
Artemis	Diana
Hermes	Mercury
Hephaestus	Vulcan
Demeter	Ceres

LYRIC POETRY

More than two thousand years ago in Greece, short poems called *lyrikos* were sung to the accompaniment of a lyre, a stringed musical instrument. Even when the poems were no longer sung, the name lyric remained.

Lyric poems are still usually short and musical. However, the main characteristic of a lyric poem is that it communicates the emotional attitude of the writer toward a person, scene, object, belief, or idea. Thus, lyric poetry is *subjective or personal* instead of *objective or impersonal*. A poet may tell a story in a lyric poem, but his or her feelings about the story are more important than the events themselves.

Over the centuries, certain types of lyric poems have become particularly well known. Among these are the song, the sonnet, and the elegy. The first two of these forms are illustrated in the following section, and the elegy is discussed in the first section (see "Break Break, Break," page 88). However, most lyric poems do not fall under any of these categories. The forms of the lyric are as varied as its infinite subjects and treatments.

WILLIAM SHAKESPEARE
(1564–1616)

"To be, or not to be—that is the question."

"Romeo, Romeo, wherefore art thou, Romeo?"

"Out, out, brief candle!
Life's but a walking shadow, a poor player
That struts and frets his hour upon the stage
And then is heard no more."

"How sharper than a serpent's tooth it is
To have a thankless child."

These lines have been spoken in theaters for more than three centuries and have been translated into many languages. Curiously, however, playgoers and scholars know more about the characters who speak them—Hamlet, Juliet, Macbeth, and Lear, respectively—than they know about the man who wrote them.

Scholars know the dates of Shakespeare's birth and death, and the place where he was born and died (Stratford-on-Avon, England). They know the name of his wife (Anne Hathaway), and the number of his children (three). However, they know little else besides the fact that he was an actor and poet as well as a playwright.

Shakespeare the actor and poet is very evident in the plays. He had the actor's ability to make characters come alive, and he wrote his plays for the most part in verse. Most of his plays are written in unrhymed verse, but rhymes occasionally appear in the plays. All of his comedies, as well as some of his tragedies, contain rhymed songs.

Shakespeare's gifts as a playwright and a poet were recognized in his own time as well as by posterity. Several years after his death, his contemporary, the poet and playwright Ben Jonson, eulogized Shakespeare as the "star of poets." And hundreds of years later, Jonson's judgment still seems correct: "He was not of an age, but for all time."

When Icicles Hang by the Wall

This is one of the two songs at the end of Shakespeare's play Love's Labor's Lost. *The first one describes spring; the second one, winter.*

When icicles hang by the wall,
    And Dick the shepherd blows his nail,°
And Tom bears logs into the hall,
    And milk comes frozen home in pail,
5 When blood is nipped, and ways° be foul,
Then nightly sings the staring owl—
        Tu-whit,
Tu-who—a merry note,
While greasy Joan doth keel° the pot.

10 When all aloud the wind doth blow,
    And coughing drowns the parson's saw,°
And birds sit brooding in the snow,
    And Marian's nose looks red and raw,
When roasted crabs° hiss in the bowl,
15 Then nightly sings the staring owl,
        Tu-whit,
Tu-who—a merry note,
While greasy Joan doth keel the pot.

2. blows his nail: warms his fingertips. **5. ways:** roads. **9. keel:** cool, or prevent from boiling over, as by skimming. **11. saw:** familiar moral saying. **14. crabs:** crab apples.

Meaning and Method

1. What descriptive words or images give an impression of the coldness of winter? Is the picture Shakespeare presents unpleasant? pleasant? both?
2. Is the owl's song merry in itself, or does it *seem* merry because it is heard from within a warm house as a meal is being prepared?

3. How do the sounds and connotations of the following words create an impression of harshness and unpleasantness?

  a. foul—owl
  b. blood is nipped
  c. birds sit brooding
  d. saw—red and raw

Why does Shakespeare want to establish an impression of unpleasantness?

Language: Onomatopoeic Words

Writers sometimes invent words to mimic the sound of something nonhuman. These *onomatopoeic* inventions (see Glossary) may not be found in the dictionary, but they serve the writer's purpose by communicating the type of sound heard and sometimes the mood it establishes. For example, in "When Icicles Hang by the Wall" Shakespeare invented the phrase *tu-whit, tu-who* to imitate the call of an owl. In "The Secret Life of Walter Mitty" James Thurber created the onomatopoeic phrase *ta-poketa-poketa-poketa* to imitate the sound made by cylinders of a ship's engine.

Invent onomatopoeic words to express the sounds emitted by the following: gale force winds, water dripping in a sink, marching of soldiers wearing heavy boots with metal taps, turning of a rusted wheel on a windmill, some other nonhuman sound.

ROBERT BURNS
(1759–1796)

Although Robert Burns lived with poverty all his life, he found a great deal in his country and people to love and celebrate in his poems. He was born in a two-room cottage in Ayr, Scotland, where his parents, tenant farmers, eked a meager living out of the thin soil. The Burns children worked hard in the fields rather than attending school, but their father communicated a love of learning to them. At every meal, young Robert sat "with a book in one hand and a spoon in the other." His mother taught him old Scottish folk stories and songs—some of which later became parts of his best poems—and he read collections of folk ballads and lyrics as he drove a cart or walked to work.

Burns continued with a life of farming after his father's death, but without success. At one point the young man was so discouraged he decided to emigrate to Jamaica. However, a volume of verse that he wrote as his "farewell" to Scotland became so successful that his life took a turn for the better, and he was able to remain.

Burns was given a minor government job, and he leased a farm. His favor with the cultured society of Edinburgh and his more secure financial position enabled him to marry his sweetheart, Jean Armour. This period, however, represented only a truce in his battle with poverty. His farm failed, and for the last five years of his life Burns struggled to support his family, becoming deeply mired in debts.

Nevertheless, out of the kind of life which might reduce others to pettiness and despair, Burns managed to sing in an uncommonly loving and lovely way of the common things and people of Scotland. His lyrics, often set to music, have been enjoyed for centuries by readers throughout the English-speaking world.

Sweet Afton*

One of Burns's sweethearts, Mary Campbell, died while they were engaged. Three years after her death, he wrote this poem, which was subsequently set to music.

Flow gently, sweet Afton, among thy green braes!°
Flow gently, I'll sing thee a song in thy praise!
My Mary's asleep by thy murmuring stream—
Flow gently, sweet Afton, disturb not her dream!

5   Thou stock dove whose echo resounds through the glen,
Ye wild whistling blackbirds in yon thorny den,
Thou green-crested lapwing, thy screaming forbear°—
I charge you, disturb not my slumbering fair!

How lofty, sweet Afton, thy neighboring hills,
10   Far marked with the courses of clear, winding rills!°
There daily I wander as noon rises high,
My flocks and my Mary's sweet cot° in my eye.

How pleasant thy banks and green vallies below,
Where wild in the woodlands the primroses blow;
15   There oft, as mild Ev'ning weeps over the lea,
The sweet-scented birk° shades my Mary and me.

Thy crystal stream, Afton, how lovely it glides,
And winds by the cot where my Mary resides!
How wanton° thy waters her snowy feet lave,
20   As, gathering sweet flowerets, she stems thy clear wave!

Flow gently, sweet Afton, among thy green braes!
Flow gently, sweet river, the theme of my lays!°
My Mary's asleep by thy murmuring stream—
Flow gently, sweet Afton, disturb not her dream!

---

* Afton: a small river in Scotland.   **1. braes** (brāz): hillsides.
7. forbear: give up.   **10. rills:** small streams.   **12. cot:** cottage.
16. birk: birch.   **19. wanton** (wŏn′tən): *here,* playfully.   **22. lays:**
songs.

Meaning and Method

1. Like the conductor of an orchestra, the speaker attempts to direct the "music" of nature. What methods does he use in lines 2 and 8 to persuade nature to let Mary sleep undisturbed?

2. What words or phrases help the speaker establish a mood of gentle sadness? Does the rhythm also contribute to this mood? In your answer, explain whether the meter is strictly patterned and even, or is varied and uneven.

3. When a speaker addresses deceased or absent persons as if they were present, or addresses an animal or thing or an abstract idea or quality as if it would understand, the speaker is said to be using *apostrophe*. Find several examples of the use of this technique in the poem, and explain what it shows about the speaker's attitude toward nature.

Ecclesiastes (3:1–8)

from THE KING JAMES BIBLE

Countless generations of writers in many countries have been inspired and influenced by the Bible. Many great works of literature are elaborations or reinterpretations of biblical stories. Moreover, the style and rhythm of biblical writing have left a strong imprint on language. The rolling cadences of the English translation of the Bible were constantly echoed in English prose. The biblical use of balanced sentences, rhetorical repetition, and metaphorical language has been widely imitated.

For every thing there is a season, and a time to every
purpose under heaven:
   A time to be born, and a time to die;
      A time to plant, and a time to pluck up that which
        is planted;

   A time to kill, and a time to heal;
5   A time to break down, and a time to build up;

   A time to weep, and a time to laugh;
      A time to mourn, and a time to dance;

   A time to cast away stones, and a time to gather stones
      together;
      A time to embrace, and a time to refrain from
        embracing;

10   A time to get, and a time to lose;
      A time to keep, and a time to cast away;

   A time to rend,° and a time to sew;
      A time to keep silence, and a time to speak;

   A time to love, and a time to hate;
15   A time of war, and a time of peace.

12. rend: tear.

Meaning and Method

1. In each line a phrase about a positive quality, such as love, is followed by a phrase about a negative quality, such as hate, or vice-versa. What does this balanced structure reveal about the speaker's view of life? Do you think the speaker is pessimistic?
2. A rhythmic effect is created in this poem by the repetition of sounds and words and by similarly structured sentences. Find several examples in the poem in which these techniques are used.

Language: Words and Expressions from the Bible

A number of frequently used words and expressions are derived from names in the Bible. Among these are the following:

1. philistine
2. wisdom of Solomon
3. a Jezebel
4. as strong as Samson
5. the patience of Job
6. good Samaritan

Use an unabridged dictionary to learn the meaning and origin of each of these words or expressions. Then write a sentence for each one.

Composition

One of the most famous biblical quotations is engraved both on a statue in a park near the United Nations headquarters and on the stairs across from the U.N. Secretariat building. It is:

> They shall beat their swords into plowshares,
> and their spears into pruning hooks;
> nation shall not lift up sword against nation,
> neither shall they learn war any more.
>
> (Isaiah 2:4)

Write a composition in which you explain **a.** the meaning of this passage and **b.** why it is an appropriate motto for the United Nations.

RICHARD WILBUR
(born 1921)

The poems of Richard Wilbur are primarily about what he calls the "things of this world"—fire trucks, a hole in the floor, grasshoppers, snow, laundry hanging on a line, the constant changes of light and shadow. Wilbur precisely observes the details which make up these things, and expresses his observations in forceful, vivid metaphors.

The son of an artist, Wilbur grew up in rural New Jersey and went on to study literature at Amherst College and to serve in World War II before he began to write poetry seriously. In 1947, the same year he received an M.A. in English literature from Harvard, he published his first book. These two almost simultaneous events established the direction his life would take, for since 1947 he has pursued the complementary careers of writer and teacher of literature at Harvard, Wellesley College, and Wesleyan University.

Wilbur is a careful craftsman who works on his poems until he feels that every word is right. The resulting verse has been awarded numerous honors, including the Pulitzer Prize for poetry in 1962. A fellow poet, Richard Eberhart, has said of him: "One of the best poets of his generation, Richard Wilbur has imagined excellence, and he has created it."

Boy at the Window

Seeing the snowman standing all alone
In dusk and cold is more than he can bear.
The small boy weeps to hear the wind prepare
A night of gnashings and enormous moan.
His tearful sight can hardly reach to where
The pale-faced figure with bitumen° eyes
Returns him such a god-forsaken stare
As outcast Adam gave to Paradise.

5

6. bitumen (bi·tōō'mən): soft coal.

The man of snow is, nonetheless, content,
10   Having no wish to go inside and die.
Still, he is moved to see the youngster cry.
Though frozen water is his element,
He melts enough to drop from one soft eye
A trickle of the purest rain, a tear
15   For the child at the bright pane surrounded by
Such warmth, such light, such love, and so much fear.

Meaning and Method

1. Why does the small boy weep? How does "his tearful sight" affect his ability to see the snowman clearly—literally and figuratively—in lines 5–8?

2. Does the snowman really return a "god-forsaken stare" or does it merely seem this way to the boy? How do the phrases *god-forsaken* and *outcast Adam* (lines 7 and 8) emphasize the boy's misery as he imagines the snowman's fate?

3. Why is the snowman content? Why does he shed a tear watching the child?

4. Why, despite the warmth, light, and love of his home, does fear surround the child? Is fear usually a part of childhood? Explain.

Discussion and Composition

Do you think the poet sees childhood as a wonderful period of life or a terrible one? or both? How do you know?

In a composition of several paragraphs, tell whether you feel that childhood is a fearful time or a happy one. Defend your statement by giving reasons and illustrative incidents from your own experience.

R. P. DICKEY
(born 1936)

R. P. Dickey was born and educated in Missouri, where he also taught briefly after graduating from the University of Missouri in 1968. Since 1969 he has taught at Southern Colorado State College and concurrently edited *Poetry Bag Magazine.*

His first book, *Running Lucky,* earned Dickey the Swallow Press New Poetry Series Award in 1969. Since then he has published a number of books of poetry and two plays.

Dickey's poems, which are often ironic, self-mocking, and rebellious in tone, have been admired for what one critic calls their "controlled casualness of style" and for the way in which they confront life honestly and without pretense. These qualities bear out Dickey's own feeling that it is the poet's responsibility to help the reader "find some hard, clear, complex, honest help in answering the question of who he is."

Shazam*

When we'd make the rounds
every couple of weeks
to trade comic books,
we'd seldom stop at George Staley's house,
5   right on the edge of downtown,
behind Goggin's Drilling Company.
He never *had* many.

But one day he climbed
to the top of Mrs. Carver's shed
10   with a towel on his back
for a cape, hollered "Shazam"
so loud Charley Sebastian could hear,

---

* **Shazam:** an interjection used to accompany the sudden appearance or disappearance of something (from *Captain Marvel* comic books).

and dove off into thin air. Actually
flew for a instant, then came
15   the crash, boom, bam that cracked
his collar bone and might have killed him
if he hadn't been so limber and fat.
George *kept* most of the comic books he had.

Meaning and Method

1. For what reason did the boys "make the rounds" every couple
of weeks? Why didn't they stop at George Staley's house? Does
he seem to be a typical boy?

2. George was ignored because the other boys felt he wasn't involved in their interests. What shows that he was, in fact, more
deeply involved in a world of adventurous fantasy than the
others? In your answer, comment particularly on lines 7 and 18.

3. Point out specific images or details which give a vivid picture of
George in the act of jumping. What does this action reveal
about him that makes us see him in a new light? Does he seem
heroic? pathetic? silly? likeable? Explain.

Compare and Contrast

Compare the child in "Boy at the Window" (p. 157) with
George Staley in "Shazam." How do the tears of one and the
leap of the other show a misunderstanding or misinterpretation of
the world around them? What aspects of childhood does each
poem emphasize? Does either poet seem to consider childhood as a
carefree time of life?

PHYLLIS McGINLEY

See biographical sketch of Phyllis McGinley on page 78.

Portrait of Girl
with Comic Book

Thirteen's no age at all. Thirteen is nothing.
It is not wit, or powder on the face,
Or Wednesday matinées, or misses' clothing,
Or intellect, or grace.
5   Twelve has its tribal customs. But thirteen
Is neither boys in battered cars nor dolls,
Not *Sara Crewe,*° or movie magazine,
Or pennants on the walls.

Thirteen keeps diaries and tropical fish
10   (A month, at most); scorns jumpropes in the spring;
Could not, would fortune grant it, name its wish;
Wants nothing, everything;
Has secrets from itself, friends it despises;
Admits none to the terrors that it feels;
15   Owns half a hundred masks but no disguises;
And walks upon its heels.

Thirteen's anomalous°—not that, not this:
Not folded bud, or wave that laps a shore,
Or moth proverbial from the chrysalis.°
20   Is the one age defeats the metaphor.
Is not a town, like childhood, strongly walled
But easily surrounded; is no city.
Nor, quitted once, can it be quite recalled—
Not even with pity.

7. Sara Crewe: child's book whose thirteen-year-old heroine, of the
same name, lives a fairy tale life, going from riches to rags and back to
riches. **17. anomalous:** doesn't conform to a general rule or to what
is expected. **19. chrysalis:** pupa or protective covering.

Meaning and Method

1. What words or phrases does the poet use in the first stanza to show that a girl of thirteen is no longer a child, but not a young woman yet either?
2. In stanza two, what actions and attitudes of the girl reveal the uncertainty and frustration of this "in-between" age? Does this description make the girl appear self-confident or unsure of herself?
3. What does the poet mean by saying that thirteen "Is the one age defeats the metaphor" (line 20)? Tell why you think this age is so difficult to characterize by a comparison.
4. The speaker is a woman, perhaps the girl's mother, who remembers what it was like to be thirteen. Does the speaker feel pity, dislike, indifference, amusement, or something else toward the girl she observes? What tells you this?

Discussion and Composition

1. What are some difficulties involved in making the transition from the "strongly walled" world of childhood to the realm of adult responsibilities and freedom? Write a paragraph explaining why adolescence in some ways means inhabiting a "no man's land."
2. What age or period of your life do you anticipate with eagerness or with dread? Why? In a poem or a paragraph, express your feelings about this age. Use at least one metaphor or simile to help show what you believe your life will be like at that time.

ARCHIBALD MACLEISH
(1892–1982)

Although many American poets in recent times have voiced strong political views, only one—Archibald MacLeish—has actually achieved a measure of political power. When appointed Librarian of Congress in 1939, the many-faceted MacLeish—a man well known for his strong liberal views—quickly became a member of President Roosevelt's "inner cabinet" of advisors. From 1944 until Roosevelt's death in 1945, he was an Assistant Secretary of State. After the war ended, he helped in the establishment of UNESCO (United Nations Educational, Scientific, and Cultural Organization).

MacLeish was born in Illinois and was graduated from Yale College and Harvard Law School. Although he practiced law for a time, poetry was his major interest, and in 1923, he sailed with his family to France in order to devote himself to writing poetry. "I date the beginning of my life from 1923," he later said about this decision. By the time he returned to the United States at the end of the twenties, he had published approximately one volume of verse a year, most of which were highly praised. In 1933, he won a Pulitzer Prize for his long verse narrative, *Conquistador.*

In 1948, after nine years of public service, he decided once again to devote most of his time to poetry, accepting an appointment as Boylston Professor of Rhetoric and Oratory at Harvard which gave him a good deal of free time to write. The time was well spent. By 1958, he had received two more Pulitzer Prizes— one for his *Collected Poems: 1919–1952,* and one for his verse play, *J.B.,* which was produced on Broadway in 1958.

Eleven

And summer mornings the mute child, rebellious,
Stupid, hating the words, the meanings, hating
The Think now, Think, the O but Think! would leave
On tiptoe the three chairs on the verandah
5   And crossing tree by tree the empty lawn
Push back the shed door and upon the sill
Stand pressing out the sunlight from his eyes

And enter and with outstretched fingers feel
The grindstone and behind it the bare wall
10 And turn and in the corner on the cool
Hard earth sit listening. And one by one,
Out of the dazzled shadow in the room,
The shapes would gather, the brown plowshare, spades,
Mattocks,° the polished helves° of picks, a scythe
15 Hung from the rafters, shovels, slender tines°
Glinting across the curve of sickles—shapes
Older than men were, the wise tools, the iron
Friendly with earth. And sit there, quiet, breathing
The harsh dry smell of withered bulbs, the faint
20 Odor of dung, the silence. And outside
Beyond the half-shut door the blind leaves
And the corn moving. And at noon would come,
Up from the garden, his hard crooked hands
Gentle with earth, his knees still earth-stained, smelling
25 Of sun, of summer, the old gardener, like
A priest, like an interpreter, and bend
Over his baskets.
                        And they would not speak:
They would say nothing. And the child would sit there
Happy as though he had no name, as though
30 He had been no one: like a leaf, a stem,
Like a root growing—

14. Mattocks: tools resembling pickaxes; **helves:** handles. **15. tines:**
spikes or prongs, as of a fork.

Meaning and Method

1. Considering the capitalization in line 3, define the tone of voice
in which the boy is spoken to. Why does he welcome the
chance to leave the house and sit quietly in the shed?
2. What does he feel, see, and smell in the shed? How does the
description in lines 6–22 indicate that the boy responds in other
ways than with words?
3. Why, in your opinion, is the old gardener compared to an
"interpreter" (line 26)? How does the gardener's attitude toward the boy differ from that of the people in the house? Why

is it appropriate that the boy's only visible friend should be a cultivator who nurtures mute, tender, growing things?

4. The people in the house expect the boy to think and to speak as other children normally do. Do you think that the similes in lines 30–31 suggest that the boy is developing, but in a way that the people in the house do not understand? Explain.

Composition

Write a paragraph describing some place whose objects, smells, and sounds have a calming effect on you, as the shed has for the boy in "Eleven." Use concrete details to help communicate the mood of the place and how you are changed by it.

MARY OLIVER
(born 1935)

Oliver was born in Cleveland, Ohio, the daughter of a school teacher. She attended Ohio State University for one year and spent another year at Vassar College. She was employed at "Steepletop," the estate of Edna St. Vincent Millay, as secretary to the poet's sister, Norma. She has been chairman of the writing department at Fine Arts Work Center, Provinceton, Mass.

Her work has been praised for its craftmanship. It has been said that she "has a great deal to offer anyone who has a capacity for being proud to be alive" and her poems are "made quietly moving by the specificity of a language demandingly her own."

She has published three volumes of verse: *No Voyage and Other Poems* (1963), *The River Styx, Ohio and Other Poems* (1972), and *Twelve Moons* (1979).

A Letter from Home

She sends me news of bluejays, frost,
Of stars and now the harvest moon
That rides above the stricken hills.
Lightly, she speaks of cold, of pain,
5   And lists what is already lost.
Here where my life seems hard and slow,
I read of glowing melons piled
Beside the door, and baskets filled
With fennel, rosemary and dill,°
10   While all she could not gather in
Or hide in leaves, grows black and falls.
Here where my life seems hard and strange,
I read her wild excitement when
Stars climb, frost comes, and bluejays sing.

9. fennel, rosemary, dill: Fennel is an herb of the parsley family. Rosemary is a shrub of the mint family; it symbolizes fidelity and remembrance. Dill is an herb of the parsley family. All three are used in cooking.

15   The broken year will make no change
      Upon her wise and whirling heart;—
      She knows how people always plan
      To live their lives, and never do.
      She will not tell me if she cries.

20   I touch the crosses° by her name;
      I fold the pages as I rise,
      And tip the envelope, from which
      Drift scraps of borage, woodbine, rue.°

      20. crosses: symbols for kisses; actually they are X's.   **23. borage,
      woodbine, rue:** Borage is a blue-flowered herb; it symbolizes courage
      and is thought to drive away sadness. Woodbine is another name for the
      Virginia creeper, a grapelike vine. Rue is a bushy herb; it symbolizes
      bitterness and grief, and also forgiveness.

Meaning and Method

1. What words or phrases in "A Letter from Home" emphasize
   the desirable qualities of the place where the speaker used to
   live?
2. What effect does Miss Oliver achieve by ending the poem with
   the word "rue"?
3. How has Miss Oliver used setting as a method of emphasizing
   the loneliness felt by the speaker?

GWENDOLYN BROOKS
(born 1917)

Most people like "tidy answers," Gwendolyn Brooks once wrote. She, however, is interested in "all the little ravelings" which others prefer to snip off or ignore. In her poems, she gently but precisely probes the often complex and knotty reactions of people to life.

Brooks, who was born in Topeka, Kansas, in 1917, was taken to Chicago shortly after her birth and has lived in that city ever since. She was educated at Wilson Junior College in Chicago, and then, after working for several years, settled down to be a wife, a mother, and a writer.

Her poetic talents, craftsmanship, and special brand of insight have been widely recognized—most notably by the Pulitzer Prize she received for her book of verse, *Annie Allen* (1949), one of several volumes of poetry. She is also the author of a novel, *Maud Martha,* a partly autobiographical account of a sensitive black girl growing up in Chicago.

One Wants a Teller in a Time Like This

One wants a Teller in a time like this.

One's not a man, one's not a woman grown,
To bear enormous business all alone.
One cannot walk this winding street with pride,
5   Straight-shouldered, tranquil-eyed,
Knowing one knows for sure the way back home.
One wonders if one has a home.

One is not certain if or why or how.
One wants a Teller now:—

10   *Put on your rubbers and you won't catch cold.*
      Here's hell, there's heaven. Go to Sunday School.
      Be patient, time brings all good things—(and cool
      Strong balm to calm the burning at the brain?)—
      Behold,
15   *Love's true, and triumphs; and God's actual.*

Meaning and Method

1. Why does the speaker want to be given advice and orders? What problems or uncertainties does the speaker mention in lines 2–3 and 7–8? How do these contrast with what he or she imagines is the adult's approach to life?
2. What is the "burning at the brain" (line 13)? Why are the italicized statements in lines 10–15 calming to the speaker?
3. The basic meter of this poem is iambic pentameter (see Glossary). Count or scan the number and arrangement of stressed and unstressed syllables in lines 1–2 to prove this statement. How do lines 5, 7, 9, and 14 depart from the basic meter? How might these shorter, more irregular lines reflect the anxieties and fears of the speaker?

Discussion and Composition

1. Are Tellers desirable in some situations and not in others? Is a combination of freedom and authority desirable? If so, which do you want more of—freedom or authority? Discuss.
2. Write a composition in which you explore a situation in which you would—or would not—like a Teller. Use concrete illustrations so that your reading audience will clearly understand why you feel, or do not feel, that a Teller would be desirable.

ARNA BONTEMPS

A biographical sketch of Arna Bontemps appears on page 58.

Blight

I have seen a lovely thing
Stark before a whip of weather:
The tree that was so wistful after spring
Beating barren twigs together.

5   The birds that came there one by one,
The sensuous leaves that used to sway
And whisper there at night, all are gone,
Each has vanished in its way.

And this whip is on my heart;
10   There is no sound that it allows,
No little song that I may start
But I hear the beating of dead boughs.

Meaning and Method

1. A blight is something that impairs or destroys. The title of the poem refers not only to the tree, but to the speaker's situation as well. How does the winter season described reflect the speaker's desolate mood? How do winter's effects contrast with spring's (described in lines 3, 5, 6, and 7)?
2. From the images in the second stanza, do you think the speaker feels he has lost hope, youth, a love, or something else?
3. Bontemps uses sounds which emphasize the meanings of his words. For example, in line 2, the repetition of the /w/ sound in "whip of weather" helps create the effect of whipping or lashing. How do the /b/ and /t/ sounds in line 4 and the /s/ sounds in lines 6–8 emphasize the meanings of these lines? Which of these sounds are harsh? Which are soft and gentle?

STERLING BROWN
(born 1901)

Sterling Brown was born in Washington, D. C., and graduated, Phi Beta Kappa, from Williams College. After completing graduate studies at Harvard in only one year, he began his career as a teacher. Most of the years he dedicated to teaching were spent at Howard University, where he served as professor of English, a position from which he is now retired.

Brown is better known, however, for his writing career, and his contributions to American literature are justly esteemed. Like Arna Bontemps, Brown has devoted his literary talents to recording the struggles of black Americans in the South. The poems in *Southern Road,* published in 1932, show a skillful handling of the themes and lyric forms common to Southern black folk songs and tales. By infusing his poems with the rhythms and stoic attitudes characteristic of that earthy folk literature, Brown captures the frustrations and tribulations felt by the black person living in the South. In "After Winter," for example, he uses language deftly to give an immediate, sympathetic picture of the man who struggles to exist within the harsh limits of the space he is allowed.

An astute critic as well as a poet, Brown has produced a number of books and articles detailing the contributions of blacks to American culture. His two most important critical works are *The Negro in American Fiction* (1937) and *Negro Poetry and Drama* (1937).

After Winter

He snuggles his fingers
In the blacker loam°
The lean months are done with,
The fat to come.

5   His eyes are set
On a brushwood-fire

2. loam: rich soil.

But his heart is soaring
Higher and higher.

Though he stands ragged
10   An old scarecrow,
This is the way
His swift thoughts go,

    "Butter beans fo' Clara
    Sugar corn fo' Grace
15   *An' fo' de little feller*
    Runnin' space.

    "Radishes and lettuce
    Eggplants and beets
    Turnips fo' de winter
20   *An' candied sweets.°*

    "Homespun tobacco
    Apples in de bin
    Fo' smokin' an' fo' cider
    When de folks draps in."

25   He thinks with the winter
His troubles are gone;
Ten acres unplanted
To raise dreams on.

The lean months are done with,
30   The fat to come.
His hopes, winter wanderers,
Hasten home.

    "Butterbeans fo' Clara
    Sugar corn fo' Grace
35   *An' fo' de little feller*
    Runnin' space. . . ."

20. **sweets:** sweet potatoes.

Meaning and Method

1. How do the farmer's actions and thoughts reflect his closeness to the land and his dependence on it? In your answer, comment on the connotations of "snuggles" (line 1) and note what things spring makes him think of (stanzas four through six.).
2. Why are the winter months called "lean"? the summer months "fat"? How do the images comparing the man to "an old scarecrow" (line 10) and his hopes to "winter wanderers" (line 31) show that winter is a difficult time for him and his family? Why is his heart "soaring/Higher" now?
3. His ten acres represent more to the farmer than a plot to raise food on. In spring they seem to offer a place where he can "raise dreams" (line 28). In what sense can he "raise dreams" on the land? Do you think the speaker agrees entirely with what the farmer thinks—that "with the winter/His troubles are gone" (lines 25–26)? Why or why not?

Compare and Contrast

How does the season affect the point of view of the speaker in "Blight" (page 170) and of the farmer in "After Winter"? In which poem does the outer condition merely reflect the inner one? In which does the season actually create the mood?

Does it seem appropriate that one poem uses formal, solemn language and the other colloquial language and dialect?

LESLIE MARMON SILKO
(born 1948)

Leslie Silko says of herself: "I grew up at Old Laguna (New Mexico) and attended BIA grade school there. Rode the bus every day 100 miles round-trip to jr. high and high school. Graduated from the U. of New Mexico in 1969 magna cum laude and Phi Beta Kappa.

"I write because I love the stories, the feelings, the words. Occasionally I think about the innovations in style and form; such thinking doesn't get a writer very far. I find publishing a big hassle with no money coming in return and people angry all the time. But I keep trying it, like Coyote* who keeps coming back for more—never quite learning his lesson." She has also said: "My writing is a gift to the Earth."

She was born in Albuquerque, New Mexico. After graduating from the university, she taught literature and creative writing there for a time. Besides poems and short stories, she has published a novel, *Ceremony* (1977).

*A mythical hero of the American Indians of the Southwest, remarkable for his resilience.

Slim Man Canyon

for John, May 1972

700 years ago
        people were living here
        water was running gently
        and the sun was warm on pumpkin flowers.
5   It was 700 years ago
        I remember
they were here
        deep in this canyon
        with sandstone walls rising high above them.
10   The rock, the silence, tall sky and flowing water
        sunshine through cottonwood leaves
        the willow smell in the wind
                700 years ago.

The rhythm,
15   the horses' feet, moving strong through
                                white deep sand.
Where I come from is like this
                the warmth, the fragrance, the silence.
Blue sky and rainclouds in the distance
20   we ride together
past the cliffs with the stories
                            the songs painted on rocks. . . .
                There was a man who loved a woman
                seven hundred years ago.

Meaning and Method

1. To the speaker, the canyon seems a peaceful place, unchanged with time, which arouses a sense of union with her ancestors. What sounds, sights, smells, and sensations does she report to create this mood? She creates the impression that the lives of ancestors reach across seven hundred years and blend with her own. How do lines 6–7, 17, and 23–24 especially help establish this bond?

2. What does the repetition of "700 years ago" (lines 1, 5, 13, and 24) emphasize in the poem? Why do you think the speaker wants to feel close to ancestors, despite the passage of a long time? Who might the *we* in line 20 be? What clue do you find in the last two lines?

3. Explain two ways "the cliffs with the stories/the songs painted on rocks" (lines 21–22) send a message across time. What is depicted on the rocks literally? What do the surroundings communicate figuratively simply by their presence?

Discussion

How are people of all times and all places alike? What emotions and appreciations do they share?

GARY SNYDER
(born 1930)

As a boy and a young man, Gary Snyder lived in close contact with the unspoiled territory of the Northwest. He grew up on his parents' farm in Washington. In the 1950s he chose work that demanded a physical involvement with nature: after a stint as a seaman, he labored as a logger, a Forest Service trail crew member, and a forest lookout in Washington and Oregon. That he found this type of work satisfying and important is evident, for the rhythms and close observations of the earth that these jobs entailed recur in many of his poems.

Following this period, Snyder lived in California and Japan, distinguishing himself in life style and poetic style from the American mainstream. He was one of a group of young California poets whose work was considered nonconformist in views and expression—the "beat" poets. His serious study of Zen Buddhist philosophy also differentiated him from most Americans.

The language of his poems is cool, firm, and exact, like the land and philosophy with which he identifies himself. Generally, the poems communicate intense sensations and a feeling of awe and wonder about common experiences. Snyder himself claims: "I try to hold both history and wilderness in mind, that my poems may approach the true measure of things and stand against the unbalance and ignorance of our times."

The Trade

I found myself inside a massive concrete shell
    lit by glass tubes, with air pumped in, with
    levels joined by moving stairs.

It was full of the things that were bought and made
5   in the twentieth century. Layed out in trays
    or shelves

The throngs of people of that century, in their style,
    clinging garb made on machines,

Were trading all their precious time
10   for things.

Meaning and Method

1. The speaker's manner of describing what he sees creates an impression that this is an alien world. How do the phrases "I found myself inside" (line 1), "things that were bought and made in the twentieth century" (lines 4–5), and "people of that century" (line 7) establish a sense of having been suddenly thrust into a strange world from another time and place?
2. The speaker is actually in a perfectly familiar place—a large department store. What are the "glass tubes," the "air pumped in," the "moving stairs," and the "things . . . Layed out in trays or shelves"? Why do you think he might want us to look at something familiar as though we were seeing it for the first time?
3. The description of objects and people is objective and direct, but it gives the impression that this society is totally mechanical. What details make the reader feel that the people are like the machines that surround them? Do you think the speaker approves of "the trade" which gives up "precious time for things"? Why or why not?
4. Each stanza is shaped with indentations that create sharp corners. How does this shape reinforce the machine-like nature of the place observed?

Discussion

The speaker in this poem values his time and considers trading it for material objects a waste of something precious. What pursuits do you consider the most worthwhile to spend your "precious time" on? Explain why you believe these activities are most valuable.

Language: Expressing Abstract Ideas in Concrete Language

Time has always been viewed as a precious commodity. Many poems have been written expressing the fascination or frustration that time's passing has for people. Because the word denotes an abstraction, or idea, rather than a tangible thing, writers have looked for concrete illustrations to give the idea of time a meaningful substance, one that can be clearly pictured. These illustrations usually take the form of metaphors, similes, or personifications. For example, different writers have expressed their views of time in these ways:

"Time, you old gypsy man"—*Ralph Hodgson*
"Time is a sandpile we run our fingers in"
                                    —*Carl Sandburg*
"Time, you thief"—*Leigh Hunt*
"Time is but the stream I go a-fishing in"
                                    —*Henry David Thoreau*
"Noiseless foot of Time"—*William Shakespeare*

In a simile or metaphor, or an apostrophe or personification, express what time is for you. Try to use concrete comparisons that your classmates would understand.

DENISE LEVERTOV
(born 1923)

Denise Levertov's early life and education were unorthodox and unusual. She was born in England and was educated "privately," primarily by random reading in her home, which she has described as "a house full of books." The variety of her education is reflected in some of the interests she chose to pursue as a young woman. She studied ballet, worked as a civilian nurse in London during the second World War, and wrote poetry (her first book of verse, *The Double Image,* was published in England in 1946).

She married an American novelist, Michael Goodman, in 1947, moved to the United States in 1948, and became a naturalized American citizen in 1956. The change of milieu had a "very stimulating" effect on her work, according to Miss Levertov, "for it necessitated the finding of new rhythms in which to write, in accordance with new rhythms of life and speech." Instead of using the traditional forms, which had characterized her British poems, she chose free forms for her American poems. Her verse shows the influence of an avant-garde movement known as "projective verse," whose practitioners believe that lines of poetry should be shaped or determined by "the breath of the poet"—that is, by the rhythms of the poet's normal speech.

The change in Miss Levertov's verse did not occur suddenly. Her second book of verse, *Here and Now* (1957), was not published until eleven years after the appearance of her first book. Since then, she has been a relatively prolific poet, producing twelve volumes of verse between 1958 and 1979.

Merritt Parkway

>   As if it were
> forever that they move, that we
>   keep moving—
>   Under a wan sky where
> 5   as the lights went on a star
>   pierced the haze & now

follows steadily
                a constant
            above our six lanes
10   the dreamlike continuum° . . .

    And the people—ourselves!
        the humans from inside the
        cars, apparent
        only at gasoline stops
15   unsure,
            eyeing each other

                    drink coffee hastily at the
                    slot machines & hurry
            back to the cars
20   vanish
                into them forever, to
                keep moving—

    Houses now & then beyond the
    sealed road, the trees / trees, bushes
25 passing by, passing
            the cars that
                keep moving ahead of
            us, past us, pressing behind us
                            and
30   over left, those that come
                toward us shining too brightly
    moving relentlessly

            in six lanes, gliding
        north & south, speeding with
35   a slurred sound—

10. continuum (kən·tin′yo͞o·əm): something that is continuous, of
which no separate parts are able to be seen.

Meaning and Method

1. The Merritt Parkway is a highway in western Connecticut, but
it could be a superhighway in any other part of the United

States. Who might be the "they" and the "we" (line 2) who move along the highway? Do you think "they" are cars? other people? What does the deliberate vagueness of these pronouns indicate about the nature of superhighways? about the speaker's attitude toward them?

2. In lines 4–10, the speaker contrasts the cars' lights with the single star that pierces the haze. How is the star different from the moving cars? What might the star symbolize?

3. Why does the speaker seem to regard the humans inside the cars as being depersonalized?

4. What are the connotations of *sealed road* (line 24)? To what literal quality of superhighways is the speaker referring in this description?

5. What words or phrases in the poem give the effect of the rushing of the cars? of their continual motion? How does the punctuation, or lack of punctuation, in the poem contribute to this effect? Why does the poem end with a dash rather than with a period? Do you think that the free verse—the particularly short line lengths and the irregular arrangement of lines on the page—is meant to contribute to this effect? If so, how?

6. What is the theme of the poem?

Composition

1. Miss Levertov wrote that William Carlos Williams "gave me instance after instance of how one's most ordinary experience could be shown in the poem as it was, invested with wonder." How does "Merrit Parkway" show the results of this "lesson" learned from Williams? In a composition, explain your answer to this question.

2. Compare the theme and style of "Merritt Parkway" and "The Trade" (page 177).

CARL SANDBURG

The experiences which lead to poetry are often fairly commonplace ones, as Sandburg (see page 50) shows in this poem.

Limited

I am riding on a limited express, one of the crack trains
    of the nation.
Hurtling across the prairie into blue haze and dark air
    go fifteen all-steel coaches holding a thousand people.
(All the coaches shall be scrap and rust and all the men
    and women laughing in the diners and sleepers shall pass
    to ashes.)
I ask a man in the smoker where he is going and he
    answers: "Omaha."

Meaning and Method

1. In lines 1–2, the speaker describes a powerful train with "fifteen all-steel coaches." What phrases or clauses in line 3 indicate that he feels that the power of the train and the happiness of the people on it are illusions?
2. What is the final destination of all the people on the train, according to the speaker? Considering this, why is the answer of the man in the smoker ironic, i.e., the opposite of what is expected?

WALLACE STEVENS
(1879–1955)

Many who read the subtle, imaginative poems of Wallace Stevens are surprised when they learn that their author worked for almost forty years as a successful insurance company executive in Hartford, Connecticut. Stevens himself professed not to understand people's surprise. "I prefer to think I'm just a man," he said, "not a poet part time, businessman the rest."

Nevertheless, although the poet and businessman were one man, the poet decidedly did not write poems in the style of business letters. In Stevens' poems, readers are told very little information directly. Instead, they are confronted by a series of impressions and seemingly unrelated statements or images. They can only understand the connections if they react to the poems, if they contribute their own interest and imagination.

The poems of Stevens, who was born in Reading, Pennsylvania, and educated at Harvard College and New York Law School, are also quite remote from the everyday world of a businessman in subject matter. His early poems were notable for their exotic, sensuous atmosphere and for their fantasy quality. Although his later poems often commented indirectly on life in the modern world, the fantasy quality remained prominent in his work.

Disillusionment of Ten O'Clock

The houses are haunted
By white nightgowns.
None are green,
Or purple with green rings,
5   Or green with yellow rings,
Or yellow with blue rings.
None of them are strange,
With socks of lace
And beaded ceintures. °

9. ceintures (san ˙torz′): belts.

10   People are not going
      To dream of baboons and periwinkles.°
      Only, here and there, an old sailor,
      Drunk and asleep in his boots,
      Catches tigers
15   In red weather.

> **11. periwinkles:** either a cone-shaped salt-water snail marked by spiral bands, or a plant with blue or white flowers (also called myrtle).

Meaning and Method

1. How does the speaker give the impression in the first nine lines of the poem that people without original, distinctive personalities live in these houses? For example, why are the houses "haunted"? Why is he disappointed that none of the nightgowns is "strange"?

2. The speaker implies that dreams of "baboons and periwinkles" (line 11) would reflect more interesting personalities. What kind of lives do dreams like these symbolize? Why might an old sailor be able to dream this type of dream? How does his life differ from the lives of the people asleep in the houses?

3. Notice the poet's use of colors throughout the poem. If white in this context suggests emptiness and lack of imagination, what does green or purple with green rings suggest? What are the connotations of the phrase *red weather* (line 15)?

Composition

By choosing unusual vocabulary and combining words in unique or striking ways, Stevens creates images to suggest the originality in personality that he admires; for example, "socks of lace," "beaded ceintures," and "red weather" would be enjoyed by someone who likes to feel different from the crowd. Make up images of your own to suggest the type of dress or dreams typical of someone with

a. a jovial, happy-go-lucky personality,
b. a quiet, sensitive personality, or
c. a pushy, self-centered personality.

JOHN MASEFIELD
(1878–1967)

From the ages of thirteen through seventeen, John Masefield served in the British merchant marine. Although he then left the sea to spend two years in New York City doing odd jobs and went on to become a professional writer, his days at sea left an enduring mark on his memory, as many of his poems show.

Masefield's vivid recollection of life at sea won much praise when his first collection of poems, *Saltwater Ballads,* was published in 1902. Encouraged by the response to the book, he began to try a variety of other types of writing. During his long life, he wrote newspaper articles, novels, short stories, verse plays, essays, and autobiographical sketches as well as verse. Yet he continued to be most admired for his poems—particularly his long narrative poems—and, in 1930, he was appointed Poet Laureate of England.

Sea Fever

I must go down to the seas again, to the lonely sea and
    the sky,
And all I ask is a tall ship and a star to steer her by,
And the wheel's kick and the wind's song and the white
    sail's shaking,
And a gray mist on the sea's face and a gray dawn
    breaking.

5   I must go down to the seas again, for the call of the
    running tide
Is a wild call and a clear call that may not be denied;
And all I ask is a windy day with the white clouds flying,
And the flung spray and the blown spume,° and the
    sea gulls crying.

8. spume (spyo͞om): foam.

I must go down to the seas again to the vagrant°
   gypsy life,
10 To the gull's way and the whale's way where the wind's
   like a whetted knife;
   And all I ask is a merry yarn from a laughing
   fellow-rover,
   And quiet sleep and a sweet dream when the long trick's°
   over.

> **9. vagrant** (vā′grənt): wandering. **12. trick:** a turn of duty at the helm.

Meaning and Method

1. For what reasons is the speaker yearning restlessly to return to life at sea? How powerful is the attraction of this kind of life for him?
2. Point out some images the poet has used in stanza one to convey the effect of the "lonely sea," and in stanza two to convey that of the "wild" sea. How does the use of /w/ and /wh/ sounds, which imitate the sound of wind, help create an appropriate mood?
3. By grouping stressed and unstressed syllables together, Masefield creates a rhythm like the rising and falling motion of the waves. For instance, line 3: "And the WHEEL'S KICK and the WIND'S SONG and the WHITE SAIL'S SHAKING." Show how he uses the same method in lines 4, 7, and 10.
4. The "long trick" in line 12 may be interpreted not only as a ship's watch, but as life itself. Keeping this second, symbolic meaning in mind, do you think that the speaker indicates in line 12 that he expects to feel satisfied when his life is over? Explain.

Discussion and Composition

The speaker of "Sea Fever" longs for the nomadic, adventurous life of a seaman. What kind of job or travel experience appeals as strongly to you as this way of life does to the sailor? In a paragraph or two, tell about the kind of life you would like to lead, explaining how the activities and responsibilities (or lack of responsibilities) of that life make it desirable to you.

BEN JONSON
(1572–1637)

Poet, playwright, actor, and scholar, Ben Jonson was a man of many talents and many contrasts. In his poems, he used the Greek and Latin classics as models and tried to imitate classical balance and harmony. In his life, however, his violent temper created havoc. Once, he was imprisoned for killing a fellow actor in a duel. At another time—when the Scottish James VI had just become James I of England—he was imprisoned for insulting the Scots.

As might be expected from his behavior, Jonson had emphatic literary opinions. He engaged in sharp battles in speech and print with many of his fellow poets and playwrights. Some poets, however, were so strongly influenced by him that they were called "Sons of Ben."

Jonson is best known for a series of bitter comedies—the most famous of which is *Volpone*—in which he attacked the greed, hypocrisy, and gullibility of his generation. However, he was also capable of creating lyrics which expressed tender feelings. Some of these lyrics are in his plays, where they are often used to show that the language of love may mask sordid intentions.

Jonson's personality antagonized many people, but his talents were widely admired. In 1616, Jonson was named Poet Laureate by James I. Although his plays are rarely performed today, in his lifetime he was considered second only to Shakespeare as a playwright. He is buried in Westminster Abbey, under a stone bearing the inscription "O Rare Ben Jonson."

Song: To Celia

Drink to me only with thine eyes,
    And I will pledge with mine;
Or leave a kiss but° in the cup,
    And I'll not look for wine.

3. but: only.

5   The thirst that from the soul doth rise,
          Doth ask a drink divine;
       But might I of Jove's nectar° sup,
          I would not change for thine.

       I sent thee late° a rosy wreath,
10   Not so much honoring thee,
       As giving it a hope that there
          It could not withered be;
       But thou thereon did'st only breathe,
          And sent'st it back to me;
15   Since when it grows, and smells, I swear,
          Not of itself, but thee.

7. Jove's nectar: Jove is one of the Roman names for the king of the gods. (The Greek name is Zeus.) Nectar is the drink of the gods. **9. late:** lately.

Meaning and Method

1. The metaphor of the first stanza shows that the presence of his love effects the speaker more pleasantly than "a drink divine" (line 6). Point out the words that extend this drinking metaphor throughout the stanza. What compliment does he pay the lady by means of the comparison? What other compliments does he pay her in stanza two?

2. What evidence indicates that the lady does not return the speaker's feelings? Why might her lack of feeling prompt him to exaggerate his compliments?

3. If you know the melody which for centuries has been sung with these lyrics, attempt to characterize it. Is it dreamy, melancholy, lively?

4. The poem's rhyme scheme and meter (number of beats or accented syllables per line) help create the classical balance and harmony that Jonson admired. What is the rhyme scheme? How do the number of beats in even-numbered lines and in odd-numbered lines balance each other?

WILLIAM SHAKESPEARE

Frances Meres, a contemporary of Shakespeare, referred to him as the "mellifluous and honey-tongued Shakespeare" and said that among his notable poems were the "sugared sonnets" which he passed "among his private friends." A collection of 154 of these sonnets—fourteen-line rhymed poems usually written in iambic pentameter—was published in 1609. Most of the sonnets were addressed to a male friend; the others were addressed to a dark-haired woman, who has come to be called the "dark lady of the sonnets."

For biographical information on Shakespeare, see page 149.

Sonnet 18— Shall I Compare Thee to a Summer's Day?

Shall I compare thee to a summer's day?
Thou art more lovely and more temperate:
Rough winds do shake the darling buds of May,
And summer's lease hath all too short a date;
5   Sometimes too hot the eye of heaven shines,
And often is his gold complexion dimmed;
And every fair from fair sometime declines,
By chance or nature's changing course untrimmed:°
But thy eternal summer shall not fade
10   Nor lose possession of that fair thou ow'st;°
Nor shall Death brag thou wander'st in his shade,
When in eternal lines to time thou grow'st:
So long as men can breathe, or eyes can see,
So long lives this, and this gives life to thee.

8. untrimmed: shorn of its beauty. **10. ow'st:** abbreviation of ownest; that is, own or possess.

Meaning and Method

1. In the first eight lines, the speaker compares his love to summer. What faults does summer have that the speaker's love, by implication, does not have? In your answer, explain the meaning of "the eye of heaven" (line 5) and "every fair from fair sometime declines" (line 7).
2. How will the speaker's love achieve a never-fading state of "eternal summer" (line 9)? How is his love immortalized? In your answer, explain the phrase "eternal lines" (line 12). In what sense will the lover remain alive and fair forever?
3. Is this poem about love? time? death? the immortality of poetry? all of these? Explain.

Compare and Contrast

This sonnet and Jonson's "Song: To Celia" (page 188) are both poems of praise. What specific qualities are being praised in each of the poems? Which praise do you find more extravagant? Why do you find it more extravagant?

JOHN CROWE RANSOM
(1888–1974)

When Ransom was a young man, most people judged poetry simply. If a poem awakened a pleasurable emotion, it was good; if not, it was bad. Ransom, who became a critic and a teacher, did much to change our way of reading poetry. He insisted that a reader should make an effort to understand the poem—to concentrate on the words and the technical devices used to communicate meaning—before judging it. Ransom was largely responsible for teaching modern readers that the first question after reading a poem should not be, "Do I like or dislike this poem?" but, "What is the poet trying to say?"

Ransom was born in Pulaski, Tennessee, and graduated from Vanderbilt University in 1909. The next year, he went as a Rhodes Scholar to Christ College, Oxford, from which he received a second B.A. in 1913. From 1914 to 1937, except for two years in the Army, he taught in the English department at Vanderbilt. In 1937, he became professor of English at Kenyon College in Ohio, and there founded and edited *The Kenyon Review,* a quarterly publication which was generally considered one of the finest literary magazines in America.

Although Ransom's activities as critic, teacher, and editor sometimes overshadowed his contributions as a poet, he is nevertheless recognized as a distinctive and distinguished poet. His style is witty and ironic, and his poems often reveal strong emotions by indirect means.

Bells for John Whiteside's Daughter

There was such speed in her little body,
And such lightness in her footfall,
It is no wonder her brown study
Astonishes us all.

5   Her wars were bruited° in our high window.
We looked among orchard trees and beyond
Where she took arms against her shadow,
Or harried unto the pond

The lazy geese, like a snow cloud
10   Dripping their snow on the green grass,
Tricking and stopping, sleepy and proud,
Who cried in goose, Alas,

For the tireless heart within the little
Lady with rod that made them rise
15   From their noon apple-dreams and scuttle
Goose-fashion under the skies!

But now go the bells, and we are ready;
In one house we are sternly stopped
To say we are vexed at her brown study,
20   Lying so primly propped.

5. bruited: talked about.

Meaning and Method

1. Which words or phrases tell you that the speaker lives in a rural area, spends some time at home, and is a neighbor of John Whiteside? What do the words *bruited, harried* and *took arms* connote about the speaker's attitude toward the girl?
2. A *brown study* usually denotes a state of absent-mindedness or reverie. How is the little girl's "brown study" different from the usual ones? What happened to her? (Consider the title and the last line.) Why is everyone so astonished at what happened?
3. What words or phrases in lines 5–16 give an impression that the girl lived in a fairy-tale world? Why might her world seem like a fairy tale to the speaker now?
4. Why is the word "vexed" (line 19) an *understatement?* (An understatement is a remark that is deliberately restrained, often to point up the significance of its contents or the situation discussed.) Are there any other understatements in the poem? Considering the situation, what might the poet have wished to avoid by using understatements?

5. What is the mood of the poem? Why is the tone or situation ironic? Consider line 7 and line 13. What could the word "shadow" symbolize?

6. In the poem, Ransom uses *slant rhyme;* that is, approximate or near rhyme. Slant rhyme is based on assonance or consonance. For example, "body" (line 1) and "study" (line 3) are slant rhymes. Find other examples of slant rhymes in the poem. Point out examples of true rhyme and explain how they differ from slant rhyme. How does the use of slant rhyme create a jarring effect, which reinforces the tone of the poem?

Language: Words with French Origins

French was extensively spoken in England after the French-speaking Normans conquered England in 1066. In the century after the conquest, a flood of words from French drastically altered the spoken and written language of England. Old English, or Anglo-Saxon (450–1150) gradually developed into Middle English (1150–1500), a stage during which many words were derived either from Old French (800–1300) or from Middle French (1300–1500). In the modern English period, which like modern French began in the sixteenth century, French additions to the English language have continued.

For example, the word "bruited" in line 5 comes from the French word *bruit,* which means "noise." As you can see, the modern English spelling and meaning are extremely close to the spelling and meaning of the modern French word. Other words and expressions that have entered our language from French are the following:

1. avant-garde	**6.** gourmet	**11.** resignation
2. couturier	**7.** hatchet	**12.** routine
3. critique	**8.** liberty	**13.** sobriety
4. elegant	**9.** margarine	**14.** unique
5. environs	**10.** palette	**15.** vignette

Look up the origin of these words in a dictionary. How close is each of these words in spelling and meaning to the original French?

EDGAR ALLAN POE

In this poem, Poe (see page 139) uses many of the sound-effect techniques of poetry to create an impression of the ringing of four different types of bells.

The Bells

I

Hear the sledges° with the bells—
    Silver bells!
What a world of merriment their melody foretells!
    How they tinkle, tinkle, tinkle,
5   In the icy air of night!
    While the stars that oversprinkle
    All the heavens, seem to twinkle
        With a crystalline delight;
        Keeping time, time, time,
10   In a sort of Runic° rhyme,
To the tintinnabulation° that so musically wells
    From the bells, bells, bells, bells
        Bells, bells, bells—
    From the jingling and the tinkling of the bells.

II

15   Hear the mellow wedding bells—
        Golden bells!
What a world of happiness their harmony foretells!
    Through the balmy air of night
    How they ring out their delight!—
20   From the molten-golden notes,
        And all in tune,
        What a liquid ditty floats

1. sledges: sleighs. **10. Runic** (roo′nik): magical or strange; runes were letters in an ancient Germanic alphabet. **11. tintinnabulation** (tin′ti·nab′yə·lā′shən): a tinkling sound.

To the turtledove° that listens, while she gloats
On the moon!
25   Oh, from out the sounding cells,
What a gush of euphony° voluminously° wells!
How it swells!
How it dwells
On the Future!—how it tells
30   Of the rapture that impels
To the swinging and the ringing
Of the bells, bells, bells—
Of the bells, bells, bells, bells,
Bells, bells, bells—
35 To the rhyming and the chiming of the bells!

III

Hear the loud alarum° bells—
Brazen° bells!
What a tale of terror, now, their turbulency tells!
In the startled ear of night
40   How they scream out their affright!
Too much horrified to speak,
They can only shriek, shriek,
Out of tune,
In a clamorous appealing to the mercy of the fire,
45 In a mad expostulation° with the deaf and frantic fire,
Leaping higher, higher, higher,
With a desperate desire,
And a resolute endeavor
Now—now to sit, or never,
50   By the side of the pale-faced moon.
Oh, the bells, bells, bells!
What a tale their terror tells
Of Despair!
How they clang, and clash, and roar!
55   What a horror they outpour

---

23. turtledove: a symbol of love. **26. euphony** (yo͞o′fə·nē): pleasant or smooth sound; **voluminously** (və·lo͞o′mə·nəs·lē): in great quantity. **36. alarum:** alarm. **37. brazen:** made of brass; also, impudent. **45. expostulation:** earnest argument; attempt to dissuade.

On the bosom of the palpitating° air!
    Yet the ear, it fully knows,
        By the twanging,
        And the clanging,
60   How the danger ebbs and flows:
    Yet the ear distinctly tells,
        In the jangling,
        And the wrangling,
  How the danger sinks and swells,
65 By the sinking or the swelling in the anger of the bells—
        Of the bells—
     Of the bells, bells, bells, bells,
      Bells, bells, bells—
  In the clamor and the clanging of the bells!

IV

70   Hear the tolling of the bells—
        Iron bells!
  What a world of solemn thought their monody° compels!
     In the silence of the night
     How we shiver with affright
75   At the melancholy menace of their tone!
     For every sound that floats
     From the rust within their throats
        Is a groan.
     And the people—ah, the people—
80   They that dwell up in the steeple,
        All alone,
     And who tolling, tolling, tolling,
      In that muffled monotone,
     Feel a glory in so rolling
85   On the human heart a stone—
    They are neither man nor woman—
    They are neither brute nor human—
       They are Ghouls:°

56. palpitating: trembling.   **72. monody** (mon′ə·dē): music in which only one person sings. In ancient Greece, a monody was a funeral song and therefore suggests sorrow.   **88. Ghouls** (go͞olz): imaginary creatures who were supposed to rob graves and eat corpses.

                    And their king it is who tolls:
90   And he rolls, rolls, rolls,
                        Rolls
                    A paean° from the bells!
                    And his merry bosom swells
                    With the paean of the bells!
95   And he dances, and he yells;
                    Keeping time, time, time,
            In a sort of Runic rhyme,
                        To the paean of the bells:
                            Of the bells:
100   Keeping time, time, time,
                    In a sort of Runic rhyme,
                        To the throbbing of the bells—
                    Of the bells, bells, bells—
                        To the sobbing of the bells:
105   Keeping time, time, time,
                        As he knells,° knells, knells,
                    In a happy Runic rhyme,
                        To the tolling of the bells,
                    Of the bells, bells, bells, bells,
110   Bells, bells, bells—
            To the moaning and the groaning of the bells.

92. paean (pē′ən): a song of praise or joy.   **106. knells:** tolls mournfully.

Meaning and Method

1. The sounds of the bells in each section create four distinct moods. Point out words in part I that help establish an atmosphere of merriment; in part II, of joy and harmony; in part III, of terror and discord; in part IV, of deep melancholy.

2. What task do the bells perform in each section? How is the type of metal assigned to the bell suitable for its task?

3. *Onomatopoeia* is a term used to describe a word which imitates a sound. For example, *tinkling* is an onomatopoeic word because it imitates the sound made by a certain type of bell. Find onomatopoeic words in lines 11, 14, and 58–59.

4. How do **a.** the /m/ sounds in part I, **b.** the /l/ sounds in part II, and **c.** the /k/ sounds in part III contribute to the mood of each part? In your answers, comment on whether the sounds involved are harsh or soft, pleasant or unpleasant.

Composition

Think of a sound which creates a mood, such as a window fan suggesting monotony or a child's laughter suggesting happiness. Write a poem, using onomatopoeic words and repetition, in which you imitate the sound and establish the mood.

THOMAS HARDY
(1840–1928)

Few writers were as strongly influenced by the area in which they lived as Thomas Hardy. Hardy's home county of Dorset in southern England is characterized by heaths—desolate tracts of open land covered with low shrubs. In most of his works, this heath country both symbolizes and dominates the bleak, tragic lives of Hardy's characters. They are unable to realize their hopes and dreams. Whether innocent or wicked, they are indifferently crushed by others or by nature itself.

Hardy won fame as a novelist—*Far From the Madding Crowd, The Return of the Native, The Mayor of Casterbridge,* and *Tess of the d'Urbervilles* are widely admired today—but refused to write fiction after the public furor over *Jude the Obscure,* published in 1896. In this book he pointed out harshly and bitterly the hypocritical differences between the Christian ideals of nineteenth-century English society and the self-righteous and destructive actions of that same society. Despite the shock and outrage of Victorian society, Hardy refused to modify the truth as he saw it, turning instead to his first literary love, poetry, which he felt would attract less public attention.

Until his death, Hardy wrote poems, most characterized by the same dark, ironic view of life found in his novels.

In Time of "The Breaking of Nations"

Only a man harrowing clods
   In a slow silent walk
With an old horse that stumbles and nods
   Half asleep as they stalk.

5   Only thin smoke without flame
   From the heaps of couch-grass;
Yet this will go onward the same
   Though Dynasties pass.

Yonder a maid and her wight°
10   Come whispering by:
War's annals will cloud into night
   Ere their story die.

9. wight: a creature; *here,* the maid's lover.

Meaning and Method

Hardy's images—a man working in a field, a pile of grass smouldering, a girl and her boyfriend passing—make the reader visualize very ordinary occurrences. Yet he says these things will endure while dynasties and wars will not. Why do you think he chose these particular images? In what sense will these things go "onward" while spectacular political struggles and empires pass and fade?

Compare and Contrast

The speaker of Hardy's poem believes that people endure through ages whereas empires crumble; the speaker of "Limited" (page 182) points out the impermanence of human life. Do you think these two poems are contradictory? Or does one poem consider human life as a continuous flow of many similar lives, whereas the other considers the lives of individuals?

SIX HAIKU*

If prizes were given to those writers who used the least number of words to communicate the greatest number of thoughts and impressions, poets would be richer than prose writers, and haiku poets would be richest of all.

The haiku (also called hokku), which was developed in Japan in the thirteenth century, is a short poem with a rigid form. In the Japanese tradition, the poem consists of three lines containing a total of seventeen syllables—five, seven, and five in each respective line. This form imposes strict discipline, requiring the poet to choose and place words carefully in order to give the expression the greatest impact in the least space. Each word suggests mood, scene, or idea powerfully. For example, the haiku poem often includes words which denote time of day or year, times which carry many associations for all readers.

These brief, contemplative poems suit the Japanese sensibility, with its commitment to the idea that "less is more." The greatest masters of haiku—frequently Zen masters as well—could, after meditation on the subject, suggest its essence with only a few strokes of the pen. Their concern was to look *as* the thing, not merely *at* it. The resulting expression, simple yet profound, opens a great range of associations for the reader, who contributes details from common experience to help create scene and mood. This imaginative participation on the part of the reader helps haiku communicate a great deal in a few words; that is, by saying less, more is suggested.

Writing haiku is difficult; translating them into a foreign language is equally difficult. In translating haiku, the strict adherence to this form is less important than capturing the spirit of the original as exactly as possible. Many fine translations of haiku have fewer or more than seventeen syllables. Harry Behn, the translator of the following selections, has managed to communicate the subtlety and depth of the haiku to the English reader.

Behn, who was born in Arizona and graduated from Harvard University, writes poems and stories primarily for children. His interest in children is apparent in his book of haiku, *Cricket Songs: Japanese Haiku,* in which he includes haiku showing "the small marvels of nature" as a child might see them.

* **Haiku** (hī′ko͞o).

1
It is nice to read
news that our spring rain also
visited your town.

—Onitsura

How do you know this poem was written to a friend? Why is the speaker happy? In your answer, discuss the connotations of *spring rain*.

2
How cool cut hay smells
when carried through the farm gate
as the sun comes up!

—Boncho

What details in this poem help you picture the scene? Is the scene static or full of motion? Does the poem indicate whether the day will be hot or cold? How can hay smell cool?

3
After the bells hummed
and were silent, flowers chimed
a peal of fragrance.

—Basho

How does this haiku show that harmony exists between the world of people and the world of nature? What words connect the flowers with the bells?

4
Broken and broken
again on the sea, the moon
so easily mends.

—Chosu

In nature, how is the moon "broken" on the sea? How does it mend? What change of mood occurs between the first and third lines of the poem? How does repetition in line 1 contribute to the original mood?

5   Tonight in this town
where I was born, my only
friends are the crickets.

—Anon.

Do you think the loneliness of this poem's speaker would have been equally great if he had found himself alone in a foreign town rather than in the town where he was born? Why or why not?

6   I must go begging
for water . . . morning glories
have captured my well.

—Chiyo

Usually one thinks of a human being as stronger than a flower. What is unusual about the attitude of the speaker in this poem toward the morning glories? In your answer, comment on the speaker's use of *begging* and *captured*. How does this haiku show the poet's love of nature?

Discussion

In his essay "Japanese Haiku," Gilbert Highet explains that the word *haiku,* "which means something like 'a beginning' . . . carries the meaning of deliberate incompleteness, or a creative activity shared between poet and reader." He lists as distinctive qualities of haiku "incompleteness, feathery delicacy of touch, sympathetic love of nature mingled with humor and tenderness, noble subjects indirectly approached." Do you agree with these observations? Do the selections included here illustrate these qualities? Give examples from several haiku to support or disprove Highet's statements.

Compare and Contrast

Compare the way in which nature is viewed in the third and sixth haiku with the way it is seen in "A Letter from Home" (page

166). Do all three poems find the natural world to be in harmony with the human world? Which poem(s) locates the human spirit *in* the objects of nature? Which poem(s) finds the life and color in nature equal and parallel to the vitality and emotions of human beings?

ELIZABETH BISHOP
(1911–1979)

Elizabeth Bishop was raised by grandparents in Nova Scotia and by an aunt in Boston, after the death of her father and the mental breakdown of her mother in 1911. She attended a boarding school in Massachusetts and Vassar College in New York, from which she graduated in 1934.

That year also marked the beginning of a friendship and the travels that were to broaden Bishop's outlook and influence her poetic style. She met poet Marianne Moore, whose poetry was the single most powerful influence on Bishop's work. She traveled in Europe, becoming familiar with many European countries, and North Africa. This openness to different cultures was also evident in her choice of permanent residence. In 1952 she moved to Brazil; from there she continued to travel widely and returned frequently to the United States.

Bishop, who has been called "our most valuable export to Brazil," was highly esteemed by her American contemporaries. She received a number of prestigious awards and grants in recognition of her poetic excellence, including a Pulitzer Prize (1956) and the National Book Award (1970).

Her poems are distinctive in their exact, meticulous descriptions and in the discipline of meter and stanzaic pattern that she imposes on her observations. These characteristics make her work seem a detached recitation of details at first. But by calling attention to its particulars, Bishop calls attention to the importance of the subject. Content with seeing clearly the beauty, pain, and sorrow of a world in process, she investigates without making judgments.

Although Bishop wrote relatively little poetry, her skill and objectivity established her as an important contemporary poet. Her poems may well endure longer than those by many writers who express cynicism or disenchantment about modern existence. As critic Anne Stevenson has noted, Bishop shows that "the world is, in spite of its confusions and injustice, a rich one, and in her poems she repeatedly strikes a clear, unwavering note of personal acceptance." *

* Quote from *200 Contemporary Authors,* ed. Barbara Harte & Carolyn Riley (Detroit: Gale Research Co., 1969).

The Fish

I caught a tremendous fish
and held him beside the boat
half out of water, with my hook
fast in a corner of his mouth.
5   He didn't fight.
He hadn't fought at all.
He hung a grunting weight,
battered and venerable°
and homely. Here and there
10   his brown skin hung in strips
like ancient wall-paper,
and its pattern of darker brown
was like wall-paper:
shapes like full-blown roses
15   stained and lost through age.
He was speckled with barnacles,°
fine rosettes of lime,
and infested
with tiny white sea-lice,
20   and underneath two or three
rags of green weed hung down.
While his gills were breathing in
the terrible oxygen
—the frightening gills,
25   fresh and crisp with blood,
that can cut so badly—
I thought of the coarse white flesh
packed in like feathers,
the big bones and the little bones,
30   the dramatic reds and blacks
of his shiny entrails,
and the pink swim-bladder
like a big peony.
I looked into his eyes
35   which were far larger than mine

8. venerable: admirable; deserving respect.   **16. barnacles:** small marine creatures usually attached to rocks or logs.

but shallower, and yellowed,
the irises backed and packed
with tarnished tinfoil
seen through the lenses
40 of old scratched isinglass.°
They shifted a little, but not
to return my stare.
—It was more like the tipping
of an object toward the light.
45 I admired his sullen face,
the mechanism of his jaw,
and then I saw
that from his lower lip
—if you could call it a lip—
50 grim, wet, and weapon-like,
hung five old pieces of fish-line,
or four and a wire leader°
with the swivel still attached,
with all their five big hooks
55 grown firmly in his mouth.
A green line, frayed at the end
where he broke it, two heavier lines,
and a fine black thread
still crimped° from the strain and snap
60 when it broke and he got away.
Like medals with their ribbons
frayed and wavering,
a five-haired beard of wisdom
trailing from his aching jaw.
65 I stared and stared
and victory filled up
the little rented boat,
from the pool of bilge°
where oil had spread a rainbow
70 around the rusted engine
to the bailer rusted orange,

40. isinglass: semi-transparent gelatin prepared from air bladders of fish. **52. leader:** device for attaching a lure or hook to a fishing line. **59. crimped:** pinched or drawn together. **68. bilge:** water that collects by seepage in a boat's bottom.

the sun-cracked thwarts,°
the oarlocks on their strings,
the gunnels—until everything
75   was rainbow, rainbow, rainbow!
and I let the fish go.

72. thwarts: rower's seats placed crosswise in a boat.

Meaning and Method

1. The poem begins with a close but impersonal observation of the fish's external surface (lines 1–21), then considers the inner workings of the fish (lines 22–47), and finally focuses sympathetically on the hooks embedded in its mouth. How do the things the speaker notices about the fish in each third reveal that she is becoming more imaginatively and emotionally involved? In your answer, point out some examples of things she observes.
2. What does the speaker recognize about the fish that makes her admire and pity it? How are the hooks "like medals with their ribbons/frayed and wavering," and the broken lines like "a five-haired beard of wisdom" (lines 61–63)?
3. What kind of victory is the speaker talking about in line 66? How has oil "spread a rainbow" in the boat, both literally and figuratively? In answering, consider the connotations of *rainbow*.

Compare and Contrast

Do you see any similarity in the attitude of the speaker in the sixth haiku (page 204) toward the morning glories and that of the speaker in "The Fish" toward the fish? Would the two speakers agree or disagree about the right of the flowers and fish to life?

Contrast the methods the poets use in expressing their attitudes toward nature; for example, how do the poems differ in the kinds and quantities of words used? Tell which method you find more effective in creating mood, and try to explain why you feel as you do.

EMILY DICKINSON

A biographical sketch of Emily Dickinson appears on page 41.

A Narrow Fellow in the Grass

A narrow Fellow in the Grass
Occasionally rides—
You may have met Him—did you not
His notice sudden is—

5   The Grass divides as with a Comb—
A spotted shaft is seen—
And then it closes at your feet
And opens further on—

He likes a Boggy Acre
10   A Floor too cool for Corn—
Yet when a Boy, and Barefoot—
I more than once at Noon
Have passed, I thought, a Whip lash
Unbraiding in the Sun
15   When stooping to secure it
It wrinkled, and was gone—

Several of Nature's People
I know, and they know me—
I feel for them a transport
20   Of cordiality—

But never met this Fellow
Attended, or alone
Without a tighter breathing
And Zero at the Bone—

Meaning and Method

1. In the first stanzas the speaker describes the movement of a
snake in the grass. With what things is the snake's movement

compared in lines 5–6 and in stanza four? How do these images convey the suddenness and briefness of its appearance?

2. The speaker feels "cordiality" for several other creatures. What effect does the snake have on the speaker? What feeling accompanies "tighter breathing" and "Zero at the Bone" (lines 23–24)?

Language: Nouns Into Verbs

The unusual manner in which a snake moves fascinates the speaker in this poem. Several of our names for animals (nouns, of course) have been "borrowed" for use as verbs to describe some activity that is similar in quality to that characterizing the animal. In each of the sentences below, explain how the verb was derived from the noun because of some distinctive quality associated with the animal it names.

a. His whip snaked through the air with a hiss.

b. She weaseled her way out of another jam.

c. The varsity team skunked their opponents last night.

d. A few boys were still larking around the park at dusk.

Composition

Dickinson described the sensation of fear as a "Zero at the Bone." Another phrase that expresses an inner physical reaction to a disappointing or fearful event is "a sinking in the pit of the stomach." What phrases can you invent to express the physical sensation accompanying the emotion of nervousness, of hilarity, of misery, of contentment?

I'm Nobody!

Dickinson's first editors changed June *in line 7 to* day. *Johnson's edition restores* June *of the original manuscript and the original placement of* Don't tell! *from line 3 to line 4.*

I'm Nobody! Who are you?
Are you—Nobody—too?
Then there's a pair of us!
Don't tell! they'd banish us—you know!

5   How dreary—to be—Somebody!
     How public—like a Frog—
     To tell your name—the livelong June—
     To an admiring Bog!

Meaning and Method

1. Is the speaker satisfied or dissatisfied at being "Nobody"? Why should being nobody be kept a secret? Who are "they" in line 4, and why would they banish those who admit to being nobody?
2. What kind of person is a "Somebody"? What is the speaker's attitude toward somebodies? How do the connotations of *frog* and *bog* emphasize her attitude?

Composition

This poem compares a "Somebody" to a frog, implying that the Somebody's self-praise is no more than a croak in a swamp. Select a different animal and write a simile comparing the quiet secluded life of the "Nobody" to that of the creature you chose. Explain in a brief paragraph why you think this simile is appropriate.

CHRISTINA ROSSETTI
(1830–1894)

Twelve years younger than her more famous brother, Dante Gabriel Rossetti, poet and painter, Christina Rossetti was born in London and educated at home. She began writing at an early age, but did not publish her verses until 1862. She was primarily a writer of devotional verse. She was a devout member of the church of England, as her mother had been. Twice, for religious reasons, she declined proposals and never married. She suffered from ill health from middle age on and gave herself over to good works and religious meditation.

She does not stand up in comparison to her American contemporary, Emily Dickinson, but is superior to any other woman writing poetry in the nineteenth century.

The First Spring Day

I wonder if the sap is stirring yet,
If wintry birds are dreaming of a mate,
If frozen snowdrops feel as yet the sun
And crocus fires are kindling one by one:
5   Sing, robins, sing;
I still am sore in doubt concerning Spring.

I wonder if the springtide of this year
Will bring another Spring both lost and dear;
If heart and spirit will find out their Spring,
10   Or if the world alone will bud and sing:
      Sing, hope, to me;
Sweet notes, my hope, soft notes for memory.

The sap will surely quicken soon or late,
The tardiest bird will twitter to a mate;
15   So Spring must dawn again with warmth and bloom,
    Or in this world, or in the world to come:
      Sing, voice of Spring,
Till I too blossom and rejoice and sing.

Meaning and Method

1. What three things are apostrophized (see Glossary) in these three stanzas?
2. What is the speaker compared to in the last line?

E. E. CUMMINGS
(1894–1962)

An innovator, experimenter, and questioner, Edward Estlin Cummings did not take the English language or its grammatical rules for granted. In his poems, he tried to shock his readers into realizing the vitality of our language by breaking rules and making his readers look at words as if they were seeing them for the first time.

For example, he changed nouns and adjectives into adverbs ("green*ly*"), adverbs into adjectives ("never*ish*"), and adjectives into nouns ("much*ness*"). To emphasize meaning, he also changed the normal arrangement of words and separated parts of words. He left out punctuation marks where they were expected, and scattered them, sometimes haphazardly, in unexpected places. Often he arranged words on a page in such a way as to create a picture of what he was describing, and occasionally he used punctuation marks as illustrations. His best-known typographical innovation was his use of small letters where capital letters were usually used and his unconventional placement of capitals where they would not normally appear—another technique which he used to reinforce the meaning of his words.

Cummings, who was born in Cambridge, Massachusetts, and educated at Harvard University, published his first volume of poetry in 1923. Its poems were romantic and traditional in subject but showed the typographical experimentation that was to become his trademark. Some recognized his important and original talent; others dismissed him as a novelty. In his lifetime, however, Cummings was accepted as a major figure in modern American poetry; some considered him the most truly delightful lyric poet in America.

In Just-   spring

in Just-
spring   when the world is mud-
luscious the little
lame balloonman

whistles   far   and wee

and eddieandbill come
running from marbles and
piracies and it's
spring

10   when the world is puddle-wonderful

the queer
old balloonman whistles
far   and   wee
and bettyandisbel come dancing

15   from hop-scotch and jump-rope and

it's
spring
and
      the

20   goat-footed
balloonMan   whistles
far
and
wee

Meaning and Method

1. What activities show that the poem describes the delight of children in spring? Why is the world described as "puddle-wonderful" (line 10)?
2. Toward what person and sound do the children come "running" (line 7) and "dancing" (line 14) from their games? Explain how the man and his sound might symbolize the freshness and gaiety of spring.
3. Considering the subject and the point of view—that of children—why might Cummings have written this poem in an open shape that seems to "tumble" down the page?

Composition

1. Write a poem or essay which parodies (see Glossary) the subject and tone of Cummings' poem by presenting the disenchanted point of view of an adult who hates walking through the spring mud and puddles.

2. Cummings describes spring as "mud-luscious" and "puddle-wonderful" to show how it appeals to children. Coin your own phrases to describe spring as it appears to teenagers, e.g., "bat-cracking-clear."

D-re-A-mi-N-gl-Y

D-re-A-mi-N-gl-Y

leaves
(sEe)
locked

5   in

gOLd
after-
gLOw

are

10   t
ReMbLiN
g

, ; : . : ; ,

Meaning and Method

1. What time of day and what time of year are being described? How do you know?

2. The first and last words of the poem use alternating capital and small letters and hyphenation or division of some letters. Explain how these techniques help emphasize the meanings of the two words.

maggie and milly and molly and may

maggie and milly and molly and may
went down to the beach(to play one day)

and maggie discovered a shell that sang
so sweetly she couldn't remember her troubles,and

5   milly befriended a stranded star°
whose rays five languid° fingers were;

and molly was chased by a horrible thing
which raced sideways while blowing bubbles:and

may came home with a smooth round stone
10   as small as a world and as large as alone.

For whatever we lose(like a you or a me)
it's always ourselves we find in the sea

5. star: starfish. **6. languid:** lacking energy or vigor.

Meaning and Method

1. According to the speaker in the last line of the poem, "it's always ourselves we find in the sea." With this in mind, explain what the things they find show about each of the girls.
2. Explain what you think the poet meant in line 10 when he described "a world" as "small," and "alone" as "large."
3. What characteristics does this poem have in common with nursery rhymes? In your answer, comment on the names of the girls as well as on rhythm and rhyme.

Composition

Write an essay of two or more paragraphs in which you describe a real or imaginary experience, such as a walk in a forest, during which you "lost yourself" or "found yourself." Try to communicate whatever in the atmosphere of the place made you forget your problems or better understand yourself.

ROBERT FROST

A biographical sketch of Robert Frost appears on page 60.

Acquainted with the Night

I have been one acquainted with the night.
I have walked out in rain—and back in rain.
I have outwalked the furthest city light.

I have looked down the saddest city lane.
5   I have passed by the watchman on his beat
And dropped my eyes, unwilling to explain.

I have stood still and stopped the sound of feet
When far away an interrupted cry
Came over houses from another street,

10 But not to call me back or say good-by;
And further still at an unearthly height
One luminary clock against the sky

Proclaimed the time was neither wrong nor right.
I have been one acquainted with the night.

Meaning and Method

1. What connotations do the words *night* and *rain* have for you?
   What frame of mind is reflected by someone who frequently
   takes long walks on rainy nights? Do you think the speaker is
   young or old, rich or poor, satisfied or dissatisfied?
2. What details in the poem indicate the isolation of the speaker
   from the life around him? Why do you think he looked down
   when he passed by the watchman? How does the speaker's
   "acquaintance" with night fit the feeling of isolation?
3. Does the punctuation at the ends of lines 1, 2, and 3 indicate
   that the poem is to be read slowly or rapidly? How does repetition contribute to the poem's pace and overall effect?

Dust of Snow

The way a crow
Shook down on me
The dust of snow
From a hemlock tree

5   Has given my heart
A change of mood
And saved some part
Of a day I had rued.°

8. rued (ro͞od): regretted.

Meaning and Method

1. What was the mood of the speaker before the incident he describes? How does it change?
2. Why is it ironic that a crow caused the day to be saved (line 7)? In your answer, comment on the connotations of *crow*. What word or phrase indicates that the bird's act might have been deliberate? Humorous?

Stopping by Woods on a Snowy Evening

Whose woods these are I think I know.
His house is in the village, though;
He will not see me stopping here
To watch his woods fill up with snow.

5   My little horse must think it queer
To stop without a farmhouse near
Between the woods and frozen lake
The darkest evening of the year.

He gives his harness bells a shake
10 To ask if there is some mistake.
The only other sound's the sweep
Of easy wind and downy flake.

The woods are lovely, dark, and deep,
But I have promises to keep,
15 And miles to go before I sleep,
And miles to go before I sleep.

Meaning and Method

1. What is implied by the fact that the "owner" of the woods lives "in the village"? Why might the speaker feel uneasy at being seen by the owner, as he indicates in lines 3 and 4?
2. Why might the horse "think it queer" that the speaker stops? Why might the horse be interpreted as a symbol of the practical side of life? of a life of action? What are the connotations of *harness bells* (line 9), and of *easy wind and downy flake* (line 12)? What contrast between two ways of life do the contrasting sounds of the bells and the weather symbolize?
3. How do you know that the speaker regrets leaving the scene? Why does he finally go on? How does his action represent a choice of a way of life?
4. Some critics have interpreted the woods as a symbol of death. What words or phrases would support such an interpretation? If the woods are a symbol of death, how might the last stanza be interpreted as a choice between life and death? Is the interpretation of the woods as a symbol of death valid? Is it better to say the woods symbolize a desire to escape from responsibility? Why?
5. The poet and critic John Ciardi has noted that Frost used a very difficult rhyme scheme in this poem. He pointed out that each four-line stanza contains three rhyming sounds and that the unrhymed sound in each stanza is used as a rhymed sound in the next stanza. The result is that one stanza seems tightly connected to the next.

Show how Frost followed this pattern in the first three stanzas. How is the last stanza both similar to and different from the others? Why might Frost have wanted to create an interlocking effect? How might the very difficulty and tightness of the rhyme scheme reflect the poem's theme?

Once by the Pacific

The shattered water made a misty din.
Great waves looked over others coming in,
And thought of doing something to the shore
That water never did to land before.
5 The clouds were low and hairy in the skies,
Like locks° blown forward in the gleam of eyes.
You could not tell, and yet it looked as if
The shore was lucky in being backed by cliff,
The cliff in being backed by continent;
10 It looked as if a night of dark intent
Was coming, and not only a night, an age,
Someone had better be prepared for rage.
There would be more than ocean-water broken
Before God's last *Put out the Light* was spoken.

6. locks: clusters or curls of hair.

Meaning and Method

1. What scene is the speaker witnessing? Point out words or images that indicate the violence of the waves and suggest that the sea and clouds are threatening the land.
2. The sea's attempt to destroy or violently dominate the land seems to symbolize to the speaker humanity's vicious attempts to destroy or dominate others. Therefore, the speaker prophesies "a night of dark intent" (line 10)—a time when evil forces of violence will dominate the worlds of both nature and people. How long will this "night" last? What effects will it have on the world?

Language: Colloquial Expressions

Colloquial expressions are words or phrases used in informal, everyday speech. Frost, for example, is using a colloquial expression when he writes that the shore was *lucky,* rather than the more literary or formal expression, *fortunate.*

What are the colloquial terms for the following "formal" expressions:

1. coiffure
2. automobile

3. motion pictures
4. stationery

DRAMATIC POETRY

In some ways, most narrative poems, and even many lyric poems, are dramatic. Like dramas or plays, they have some or all of the following elements: settings, characters, dialogue, action, and emotional conflict. The term *dramatic poetry,* however, applies to a specific type of poem—one in which the speaker has a definite personality which is obviously not that of the poet. (The distinction between the speaker and the poet is obvious when, for example, the poet speaks from the point of view of a member of the opposite sex, of a dead person, or of someone with a different name.) The main purpose of dramatic poems is to reveal character, generally at a moment of conflict.

A dramatic poem always has at least one speaker who talks to someone else. The other person or persons may or may not answer, but another presence is always mentioned in the poem.

Dramatic poetry deals with a moment of conflict or stress which causes characters to reveal their "true" selves as they react to it. This process is particularly evident in the *dramatic monologue,* in which only one person talks (*mono* is the Greek word for "one"). In dramatic monologues, the speakers often reveal their characters by seeming to think aloud about their problems. They usually answer questions or objections that they think up, or that they imagine their listeners to be asking silently.

RUDYARD KIPLING

In this poem, Kipling (see page 120) presents a dialogue between two soldiers in the British Army. Both soldiers speak in the
cockney dialect of East London.

Danny Deever

"What are the bugles blowin' for?" said Files-on-Parade.°
"To turn you out, to turn you out," the Color-Sergeant°
said.
"What makes you look so white, so white?" said
Files-on-Parade.
"I'm dreadin' what I've got to watch," the Color-Sergeant
said.

5 For they're hangin' Danny Deever, you can 'ear
  the Dead March play,
 The regiment's in 'ollow square°—they're hangin' him
  today;
 They've taken of his buttons off an' cut his stripes away
 An' they're hangin' Danny Deever in the mornin'.

"What makes the rear-rank breathe so 'ard?" said
Files-on-Parade.
10 "It's bitter cold, it's bitter cold," the Color-Sergeant said.
"What makes that front-rank man fall down?" said
Files-on-Parade.
"A touch of sun, a touch of sun," the Color-Sergeant said.
 They are hangin' Danny Deever, they are marchin'
  of 'im round.
 They 'ave 'alted Danny Deever by 'is coffin
  on the ground:
15 An' 'e'll swing in 'arf a minute for a sneakin', shootin'
  hound—
 O they're hangin' Danny Deever in the mornin'!

1. **Files-on-Parade:** the soldier who directs marching formation.
(A file is a line of soldiers.) 2. **Color-Sergeant:** the flag-bearer.
6. **'ollow square:** At a hanging, the ranks of soldiers form three sides
of a square; the fourth side is the gallows.

"'Is cot was right-'and cot to mine," said Files-on-Parade.
"'E's sleepin' out an' far tonight," the Color-Sergeant said.
"I've drunk 'is beer a score o' times," said Files-on-Parade.

20   "'E's drinkin' bitter beer alone," the Color-Sergeant said.
     They are hangin' Danny Deever, you must mark 'im
        to 'is place,
     For 'e shot a comrade sleepin'—you must look 'im
        in the face;
     Nine 'undred of 'is county an' the regiment's disgrace,
     While they're hangin' Danny Deever in the mornin'.

25   "What's that so black agin the sun?" said
        Files-on-Parade.
     "It's Danny fightin' 'ard for life," the Color-Sergeant said.
     "What's that that whimpers over'ead?" said
        Files-on-Parade.
     "It's Danny's soul that's passin' now," the Color-Sergeant
        said.
     For they're done with Danny Deever, you can 'ear
        the quickstep play,

30   The regiment's in column, an' they're marchin' us
        away;
     Ho! the young recruits are shakin', an' they'll want
        their beer today,
     After hangin' Danny Deever in the mornin'.

Meaning and Method

1. What details and comments show that the Color-Sergeant is
   distressed by the hanging? Why is Files-on-Parade sympathetic
   to Danny Deever?
2. How do the soldiers react to the hanging? Do the Color-
   Sergeant's statements in lines 9–12 explain their reactions realis-
   tically, or is he making up reasons to avoid saying what really
   causes their response?
3. Do the soldiers seem to feel distressed because they feel Danny
   Deever does not deserve to be hanged or because witnessing the
   hanging horrifies them?

4. Kipling alternates sentences of dialogue in a way that creates a mechanical effect; he also uses the rhythm and musical echoes of a march throughout the poem. How do these techniques emphasize the movement and mood of the speakers?

Composition

Write a composition in which you defend or attack the type of justice meted out by the army to Danny Deever. Or write a composition in which you explain whether you think capital punishment—the death penalty for a crime—is ever justified. Give reasons for your opinions.

ALFRED, LORD TENNYSON

Tennyson (see page 87) said that he wrote this poem after the death of his friend, Arthur Hallam, to describe his "feeling about the need of going forward. . . ." He drew his subject from two ancient Greek epics, the *Iliad* and the *Odyssey*.

The *Iliad* begins near the end of a ten-year war in Troy, in Asia Minor, between the Greeks and the Trojans, and describes the gods and the heroic figures on both sides who took part in this war. The *Odyssey* is devoted to the fantastic adventures and misadventures of the Greek hero Odysseus—called Ulysses by the Romans—in his ten-year attempt to reach home after the Trojan War had ended. It ends with his return to Ithaca, the island off the Greek mainland over which he ruled, and his reunion with his faithful wife, Penelope.

Tennyson began his poem where the *Odyssey* left off, imagining Ulysses three years after his return to Ithaca.

Ulysses

It little profits that an idle king,
By this still hearth, among these barren crags,
Matched with an aged wife, I mete and dole°
Unequal laws unto a savage race,
5   That hoard, and sleep, and feed, and know not me.
I cannot rest from travel: I will drink
Life to the lees.° All times I have enjoyed
Greatly, have suffered greatly, both with those
That loved me, and alone; on shore, and when
10   Through scudding° drifts the rainy Hyades°
Vexed the dim sea. I am become a name;
For always roaming with a hungry heart
Much have I seen and known—cities of men
And manners, climates, councils, governments,
15   Myself not least, but honored of them all—

3. mete and dole: measure and give out. **7. lees:** dregs, usually of wine, which settle to the bottom of a cup. **10. scudding:** rushing or moving swiftly; **Hyades** (hī′ə·dēz): "rainy ones" in Greek; stars in the constellation Taurus, whose appearance signaled the rainy season.

And drunk delight of battle with my peers,
Far on the ringing plains of windy Troy.
I am a part of all that I have met;
Yet all experience is an arch wherethrough
20 Gleams that untraveled world whose margin fades
Forever and forever when I move.
How dull it is to pause, to make an end,
To rust unburnished,° not to shine in use!
As though to breathe were life. Life piled on life
25 Were all too little, and of one to me
Little remains: but every hour is saved
From that eternal silence, something more,
A bringer of new things; and vile it were
For some three suns to store and hoard myself,
30 And this gray spirit yearning in desire
To follow knowledge, like a sinking star,
Beyond the utmost bound of human thought.
　　　This is my son, mine own Telemachus,°
To whom I leave the scepter and the isle—
35 Well-loved of me, discerning to fulfill
This labor, by slow prudence to make mild
A rugged people, and through soft degrees
Subdue them to the useful and the good.
Most blameless is he, centered in the sphere
40 Of common duties, decent not to fail
In offices of tenderness, and pay
Meet° adoration to my household gods,°
When I am gone. He works his work, I mine.
　　　There lies the port; the vessel puffs her sail:
45 There gloom the dark broad seas. My mariners,
Souls that have toiled, and wrought, and thought
　　　with me—
That ever with a frolic welcome took
The thunder and the sunshine, and opposed°
Free hearts, free foreheads—you and I are old;
50 Old age hath yet his honor and his toil.

23. unburnished: unpolished; to burnish is to polish by means of friction. **33. Telemachus** (tə‧lemʹə‧kəs): Ulysses' son, who by this time is old enough to rule. **42. Meet:** proper; **household gods:** special gods, generally the souls of ancestors, who were supposed to watch over each house. **48. opposed:** *here,* fought with.

Death closes all; but something ere the end,
Some work of noble note, may yet be done,
Not unbecoming men that strove with gods.
The lights begin to twinkle from the rocks:
55 The long day wanes; the slow moon climbs; the deep
Moans round with many voices. Come, my friends,
'Tis not too late to seek a newer world.
Push off, and sitting well in order smite
The sounding furrows; for my purpose holds
60 To sail beyond the sunset, and the baths
Of all the western stars, until I die.
It may be that the gulfs will wash us down:
It may be we shall touch the Happy Isles,°
And see the great Achilles,° whom we knew.
65 Though much is taken, much abides; and though
We are not now that strength which in old days
Moved earth and heaven, that which we are, we are,—
One equal temper of heroic hearts,
Made weak by time and fate, but strong in will
70 To strive, to seek, to find, and not to yield.

63. Happy Isles: in Greek mythology, the home of heroes after death (also called the Elysian Fields). **64. Achilles** (ə·kil′ēz): a Greek hero of the Trojan War who was killed before the war ended.

Meaning and Method

1. Ulysses speaks to the men with whom he sailed before, urging them to return to their quest of the "untraveled world." Why isn't he satisfied with the memory of his earlier adventures? What is the gleaming "untraveled world" whose margin always fades before him (lines 19–21)?
2. What great goal in life does Ulysses express in lines 30–32? Find evidence that his desire for travel represents something more than wanderlust or a yearning for adventure.
3. How does Ulysses differ from his son Telemachus (described in lines 33–43) and from his people (described in lines 4–5 and 37–38)? Do you think he feels superior to them? Why or why not?

4. What is Ulysses' attitude toward old age, as expressed in lines 50–53 and 65–70?
5. Reread the definition of *dramatic monologue* on page 225. Is "Ulysses" a dramatic monologue? Why or why not?

Discussion and Composition

Do you think that Ulysses is noble, or is he selfish and deliberately avoiding responsibilities? In a composition or a class discussion, give reasons for your point of view.

MARGARET ATWOOD
(born 1939)

Margaret Atwood was born in Ottawa, Canada and has degrees from the University of Toronto and Radcliffe College of Harvard University. Her first book of poetry won the prestigious Governor General's Award. She was 27—the youngest person ever to receive this award. She has taught in several universities, but now devotes her entire time to writing. Besides her many books of verse she has also written four novels: *The Edible Woman, Surfacing, Lady Oracle,* and *Life Before Man.* She has also written a "thematic guide" to Canadian literature. She is very interested in mythology and frequently writes on mythological subjects.

Siren Song*

This is the one song everyone
would like to learn: the song
that is irresistible:

the song that forces men
5   to leap overboard in squadrons
even though they see the beached skulls

the song nobody knows
because anyone who has heard it
is dead, and the others can't remember.

10   Shall I tell you the secret
and if I do, will you get me
out of this bird suit?

I don't enjoy it here
squatting on this island
15   looking picturesque and mythical

* **Siren:** one of three sea nymphs, part woman and part bird, who had the power of charming and destroying all who heard her.

with these two feathery maniacs,
I don't enjoy singing
this trio, fatal and valuable.

I will tell the secret to you,
20   to you, only to you.
Come closer. This song

is a cry for help: Help me!
Only you, only you can,
you are unique

25   at last. Alas
it is a boring song
but it works every time.

Meaning and Method

1. What might the "beached skulls" represent in line 6?
2. Given the classical, mythological setting of this poem, what is incongruous (out of keeping) in the phrase "bird suit"? How does line 15 undermine the whole classical setting? What other phrases are jarringly modern? Are they humorous?
3. What dramatic reversal happens in the last line? Do you believe that the siren's request is genuine? What do you think happened to her listener at the end of the poem?

ROBERT BROWNING
(1812–1889)

The dramatic monologues written by Robert Browning have been and are greatly admired. Browning, who experimented with and became a master of this form, proved that these dramatic poems could bring powerful characters to life in subtle ways. His best monologues not only create realistic, complex characters, they also capture the speech patterns and jumps in thought that are natural to someone speaking at length to someone else. They show a deep understanding of human nature and motivation, and create the impression that the reader is actually listening to a real person. They are made even richer by Browning's choice of characters—frequently Renaissance artists or thinkers—who naturally express their views in language that appeals to the senses, stressing colors, shapes, and textures.

This flair for the dramatic was evident in Browning's personal life as well. After reading the poems of Elizabeth Barrett, Browning resolved to meet the invalid poet. At first Miss Barrett, who was virtually imprisoned in her London home by a tyrannical father, refused to see him. Their romance flourished in their letters to one another. Browning persisted until he not only met Elizabeth, but persuaded her to marry him, despite the disapproval of her father. In 1846 the two poets eloped and moved to Florence, Italy, the city that was to be their home until Mrs. Browning died in 1861.

Although he wrote steadily throughout his adult life, Browning was past fifty before he received the recognition he deserved. His methods and subjects were atypical for his time; while most poets were writing sweet lyrics or moralistic poems, Browning wrote poems probing the psychological motivations of complex individuals. The Victorian public also found the irregular rhythms, the condensed thoughts, and the jumps in thought that Browning used in his monologues different from the poetic tradition they appreciated.

It was not until 1868, with the publication of his long verse narrative *The Ring and the Book,* that he was finally recognized as a poet equal in stature to the giant of Victorian poetry, Alfred, Lord Tennyson, the Poet Laureate.

My Last Duchess

FERRARA*

*The duke is arranging for a second marriage, to a count's
daughter. As he shows the count's emissary his palace and art
objects, attempting to make a favorable impression, he reveals more
of his true character than he intends.*

That's my last duchess painted on the wall,
Looking as if she were alive. I call
That piece a wonder, now: Frà Pandolf's° hands
Worked busily a day, and there she stands.
5   Will't please you sit and look at her? I said
"Frà Pandolf" by design, for never read
Strangers like you that pictured countenance,°
The depth and passion of its earnest glance,
But to myself they turned (since none puts by
10   The curtain I have drawn for you, but I)
And seemed as they would ask me, if they durst,°
How such a glance came there; so, not the first
Are you to turn and ask thus. Sir, 'twas not
Her husband's presence only, called that spot
15   Of joy into the Duchess' cheek: perhaps
Frà Pandolf chanced to say "Her mantle laps
Over my lady's wrist too much," or "Paint
Must never hope to reproduce the faint
Half-flush that dies along her throat": such stuff
20   Was courtesy, she thought, and cause enough
For calling up that spot of joy. She had
A heart—how shall I say?—too soon made glad,
Too easily impressed; she liked whate'er
She looked on, and her looks went everywhere.
25   Sir, 'twas all one! My favor at her breast,
The dropping of the daylight in the West,
The bough of cherries some officious° fool

---

* **Ferrara:** a city in northern Italy which was a center of art and culture during the Renaissance.   **3. Frà Pandolf:** an imaginary Renaissance painter.   **7. countenance:** face or expression.   **11. durst:** dared.
27. officious: eager to be of service.

Broke in the orchard for her, the white mule
She rode with round the terrace—all and each
30 Would draw from her alike the approving speech,
Or blush, at least. She thanked men—good! but thanked
Somehow—I know not how—as if she ranked
My gift of a nine-hundred-years-old name
With anybody's gift. Who'd stoop to blame
35 This sort of trifling? Even had you skill
In speech—which I have not—to make your will
Quite clear to such an one, and say, "Just this
Or that in you disgusts me; here you miss,
Or there exceed the mark"—and if she let
40 Herself be lessoned so, nor plainly set
Her wits to yours, forsooth, and made excuse,
—E'en then would be some stooping; and I choose
Never to stoop. Oh sir, she smiled, no doubt,
Whene'er I passed her; but who passed without
45 Much the same smile? This grew; I gave commands;
Then all smiles stopped together. There she stands
As if alive. Will 't please you rise? We'll meet
The company below, then. I repeat,
The Count your master's known munificence°
50 Is ample warrant that no just pretense
Of mine for dowry° will be disallowed;
Though his fair daughter's self, as I avowed
At starting, is my object. Nay, we'll go
Together down, sir. Notice Neptune,° though,
55 Taming a sea-horse, thought a rarity,
Which Claus of Innsbruck° cast in bronze for me!

49. munificence: generosity. **51. dowry:** money, goods, or estate a
woman brings to her husband in marriage. **54. Neptune:** Roman god
of the sea. **56. Claus of Innsbruck:** imaginary Renaissance sculptor.

Meaning and Method

1. What do lines 8 and 23–24 show about the duchess' character?
   What do you think caused her death?
2. The duke's comments about his "last duchess" reveal a great
   deal about his character. What did he expect from her? Why
   was it unacceptable to him that she "liked whate'er/She looked

on" (lines 23–24) and was just as happy about the gift of a "bough of cherries" (line 27) as about his "gift of a nine-hundred-years-old name" (line 33)?

3. Would you characterize the duke as loving or excessively possessive? maniacally proud or justifiably concerned about his social position? Point out lines of his monologue that support your choices.

4. How does the statue of Neptune "taming a sea-horse" (line 55) symbolize the duke's relationships with people? In what way are his attitudes toward art and women alike?

5. This poem is written in iambic pentameter couplets (each two lines rhyme and every line contains five two-syllable beats), yet its effect is conversational. Locate uses of punctuation and *enjambment* (lines whose thought continues beyond the end of the line) which help create this effect.

Discussion and Composition

1. What is the duke's opinion of himself? What is your characterization of him? In a composition or a discussion, tell how the two attitudes differ and why you cannot see the duke as he sees himself.

2. Discuss the Renaissance marriage customs and attitudes toward social class and art, as revealed in "My Last Duchess." How did their customs and attitudes differ from ours?

The
Epic

EPIC POETRY

Epics, which were originally long narrative poems about the exploits of a national hero or heroes, are found in many lands and in many languages. For example, the English have the epic *Beowulf* (written in Old English, or Anglo-Saxon), and the French have *The Song of Roland*. The oldest existing epics in the western world are the Greek epics, the *Iliad* and the *Odyssey*.

Folk epics, like folk ballads, were composed in the days before printing. Although the ones which survived were eventually written down, they were first spread by wandering bards who sang or recited them. Some of these epics are so long that it is hard to believe that anyone could have sung them from memory. Most likely, they were not memorized word for word. The singers had to know the basic stories, but could add or delete details. They could also interpret the stories as they chose, emphasizing certain parts and playing down others to bring out the points they wished to make.

Epics were usually based on actual events, but these events and the people who took part in them became interwoven with the supernatural as the deeds were told and retold. In the Greek epics, for example, the gods and goddesses helped or hindered the heroes, and constantly appeared on earth in various disguises. The gods and goddesses were themselves like super-mortals: they played favorites, fell in and out of love, and quarreled with one another, often producing enormous catastrophes for human beings as a result.

The epic poets, like the people to whom they sang, saw human qualities in gods, magic in ordinary things, and godlike qualities in human beings. The world of the epics is a world which existed before science had been conceived, before things had been diagnosed and classified. It is a world not unlike the world of a child, where the dark hides unknown terrors, the woods may conceal monsters, and everything is both more beautiful and terrible than adults can imagine.

Homer

No facts are known about Homer, the Greek poet who is traditionally credited with having written both the *Iliad* and the *Odyssey*. It is believed that he lived in Asia Minor in the eighth or ninth century B.C. According to legend, he was a blind poet who wandered from place to place reciting his epics. In his own day, and for generations afterward, he was considered by the Greeks to be divinely inspired.

Many scholars think that the stories in the Homeric epics had been sung about separately for centuries before Homer was born, but that Homer wove these legends together, rejecting some parts, unifying the whole, and presenting the characters and events from his own point of view.

The real war on which Homer's epic, the *Iliad,* is based took place at the end of the twelfth century B.C. and is believed to have been a trade war between the Greeks and their Asia Minor rivals, the Trojans. Homer, probably following previous legends, ignored the economic motive for the devastating ten-year-long war. Instead, he presented the war as the direct result of the abduction of Helen, the beautiful wife of the Greek king of Lacedaemon, Menelaus, by the Trojan prince Paris. He also presented the war as being ultimately caused by a rivalry among the gods, rather than a human event. The *Iliad* is a moving illustration of the theme that even the greatest heroes are prey not only to their human weaknesses but also to powers over which they have no control. Betrayal and tragedy are the rewards for the heroes in the *Iliad*.

The *Odyssey,* a very different type of epic, is about the trials and adventures of Odysseus, one of the Greek kings who plays a prominent part in the *Iliad*. The *Odyssey* relates the wanderings of Odysseus after the Trojan War had ended with a Greek triumph. According to Homer, Odysseus was prevented by the angry gods from returning home for ten years because the Greeks, on their last day in Troy, had pillaged and burned the temples of the gods.

The *Odyssey* is a fantastic story. Odysseus and his men meet giants, enchantresses, sea monsters, and ghosts who materialize after drinking blood. However, many of the details in the story are realistic and show much about the life of the Homeric and pre-Homeric Greeks. For example, we see the primitive rural life of one of the giants, a man-eater who milks goats and makes cheese. Throughout the *Odyssey,* we get a feeling of the terror of seamen who were at the mercy of wind and waves in boats powered by oars and sails, and who were forced to land on unknown islands in order to get food for their survival. In this realistic fantasy, unlike the *Iliad,* the strong human being triumphs, though with the aid of the gods. Odysseus returns home in time to save his faithful wife, Penelope, from the suitors she had warded off for twenty years and regains his kingdom.

Since Homer wrote in Greek, much of the impact—or lack of impact—of his work on the English-speaking reader is due to the translator. The translator of the following selection is Robert Fitzgerald, a poet as well as a classical scholar, who has turned Homer's Greek into vivid and vibrant English poetry.

THE ODYSSEY

The Odyssey, *which is composed of twenty-four parts, begins near the end of Odysseus' voyage. However, because Odysseus tells of his past adventures, we find out about all the strange sights he has seen and the perils he has endured during his long voyage. The selection presented here, which includes parts of books nine and twelve, opens when Odysseus begins relating his experiences to a friendly king.*

The following is a list of characters encountered in this excerpt:

Characters
(in alphabetical order)

AEOLUS (ē ə· ləs): *king of the winds.*

CALYPSO (kə· lip'sō): *a nymph on whose island Odysseus and his men were shipwrecked. She kept him from leaving her for seven years but finally allowed him to go.*

CHARYBDIS (kə· rib'dis): *a monster who lived in a whirlpool. See* **Scylla.**

CICONES (si· kōn'ēz): *a people in whose country Odysseus and his men landed.*

CIRCE OF AIAIA (sûr'sē; ē'ē·ə): *an enchantress who changed Odysseus' sailors into swine.*

CYCLOPES (sī· klō'pēz): *a mythical race of giants who had only one eye each in the middle of their foreheads. They were supposedly descended from Poseidon, god of the sea.*

CYCLOPS (sī'klops): *one of the Cyclopes. See* **Polyphemos.**

LAESTRYGONES (les· trig'on· ēz): *a tribe of man-eaters.*

LOTUS EATERS: *a people who lived an indolent, drugged life.*

ODYSSEUS (ō· dis'yōos): *Greek king of Ithaca, hero of the Odyssey.*

POLYPHEMOS (pol'i· fē'məs): *the one Cyclops whom Odysseus and his men encountered; he is usually referred to simply as Cyclops.*

SCYLLA (sil'e): *a six-headed sea monster. Odysseus and his men had to pass between Scylla and Charybdis, two great horrors.*

SIRENS: *three sea nymphs who were part woman, part bird. They lured sailors to their deaths on rocky coasts by their singing.*

"I am Laertes'° son, Odysseus.

Men hold me
formidable for guile in peace and war:
this fame has gone abroad to the sky's rim.
My home is on the peaked sea-mark° of Ithaca
5   under Mount Neion's° wind-blown robe of leaves,
in sight of other islands—Doulikhion,°
Same,° wooded Zakynthos°—Ithaca
being most lofty in that coastal sea,
and northwest, while the rest lie east and south.
10   A rocky isle, but good for a boy's training;
I shall not see on earth a place more dear,
though I have been detained long by Calypso,
loveliest among goddesses, who held me
in her smooth caves, to be her heart's delight,
15   as Circe of Aiaia, the enchantress,
desired me, and detained me in her hall.
But in my heart I never gave consent.
Where shall a man find sweetness to surpass
his own home and his parents? In far lands
20   he shall not, though he find a house of gold.

1. **Laertes** (lā·ûr′tēz).   4. **sea-mark:** an elevated object which sailors
use to guide them.   5. **Mount Neion** (nē·ī′ən).   6. **Doulikhion**
(dōō·lik′ē·on).   7. **Same** (sā′mē); **Zakynthos** (zā·kin′thos).

(*Odysseus then describes landing in the country of the Cicones,
where he and his men took plunder and enslaved the women. They stayed
too long, however, and had to battle the army of the Cicones, losing a
number of men in the process. Back at sea, they faced a storm that lasted for
nine days.*)

THE LOTUS EATERS

Nine days I drifted on the teeming sea
before dangerous high winds. Upon the tenth
we came to the coastline of the Lotus Eaters,
who live upon that flower.° We landed there
25   to take on water. All ships' companies

24. **that flower:** the lotus, which induced forgetfulness and a mood of
tranquillity.

mustered alongside for the mid-day meal.
Then I sent out two picked men and a runner
to learn what race of men that land sustained.
They fell in, soon enough, with Lotus Eaters,
30   who showed no will to do us harm, only
offering the sweet Lotus to our friends—
but those who ate this honeyed plant, the Lotus,
never cared to report, nor to return:
they longed to stay forever, browsing on
35   that native bloom, forgetful of their homeland.
I drove them, all three wailing, to the ships,
tied them down under their rowing benches,
and called the rest: 'All hands aboard;
come, clear the beach and no one taste
40   the Lotus, or you lose your hope of home.'
Filing to their places by the rowlocks
my oarsmen dipped their long oars in the surf,
and we moved out again on our seafaring.

Meaning and Method

What effect does the lotus flower have on people who eat it?
What might this flower symbolize? What difference between
Odysseus and his men is shown by his act of driving them back to
the ships?

THE CYCLOPES

In the next land we found were Cyclopes,
45   giants, louts, without a law to bless them.
In ignorance leaving the fruitage of the earth
    in mystery
to the immortal gods, they neither plow
nor sow by hand, nor till the ground, though grain—
wild wheat and barley—grows untended, and
50   wine-grapes, in clusters, ripen in heaven's rain.
Cyclopes have no muster and no meeting,°
no consultation or old tribal ways,

51. no muster and no meeting: no institutions to make laws or community decisions.

but each one dwells in his own mountain cave
dealing out rough justice to wife and child,
55   indifferent to what the others do.

(*Before crossing to the land of the Cyclopes, Ulysses and his men had
spent the night on a nearby desert island. He describes the island, and tells
how he prepared to enter the Cyclopes' territory, which lay across the bay.*)

When the young Dawn with finger tips of rose
came in the east, I called my men together
and made a speech to them:
                              'Old shipmates, friends,
the rest of you stand by; I'll make the crossing
60   in my own ship, with my own company,
and find out what the mainland natives are—
for they may be wild savages, and lawless,
or hospitable and god-fearing men.'

At this I went aboard, and gave the word
65   to cast off by the stern. My oarsmen followed,
filing in to their benches by the rowlocks,
and all in line dipped oars in the grey sea.

As we rowed on, and nearer to the mainland,
at one end of the bay, we saw a cavern
70   yawning above the water, screened with laurel,
and many rams and goats about the place
inside a sheepfold—made from slabs of stone
earthfast° between tall trunks of pine and rugged
towering oak trees.
                     A prodigious° man
75   slept in this cave alone, and took his flocks
to graze afield—remote from all companions,
knowing none but savage ways, a brute
so huge, he seemed no man at all of those
who eat good wheaten bread; but he seemed rather
80   a shaggy mountain reared in solitude.
We beached there, and I told the crew

---

73. earthfast: stuck in the earth.   **74. prodigious** (prə·dij′əs): enormous; *here,* like a monster.

to stand by and keep watch over the ship;
as for myself I took my twelve best fighters
and went ahead. I had a goatskin full
85   of that sweet liquor that Euanthes'° son
Maron,° had given to me. He kept Apollo's°
holy grove at Ismaros;° for kindness
we showed him there, and showed his wife and child,
he gave me seven shining golden talents°
90   perfectly formed, a solid silver winebowl,
and then this liquor—twelve two-handled jars
of brandy, pure and fiery. Not a slave
in Maron's household knew this drink; only
he, his wife and the storeroom mistress knew;
95   and they would put one cupful—ruby-colored,
honey-smooth—in twenty more of water,
but still the sweet scent hovered like a fume
over the winebowl. No man turned away
when cups of this came round.
                         A wineskin full
100   I brought along, and victuals in a bag,
for in my bones I knew some towering brute
would be upon us soon—all outward power,
a wild man, ignorant of civility.

We climbed, then, briskly to the cave. But Cyclops
105   had gone afield, to pasture his fat sheep,
so we looked round at everything inside:
a drying rack that sagged with cheeses, pens
crowded with lambs and kids, each in its class:
firstlings apart from middlings, and the 'dewdrops,'
110   or newborn lambkins, penned apart from both.
And vessels full of whey° were brimming there—
bowls of earthenware and pails for milking.
My men came pressing round me, pleading:

85. Euanthes (yōō·an′thēz).   **86. Maron** (mā′rən);   **Apollo**
(ə·pol′ō): the Greek god of music, poetry, medicine, prophecy, and of
the sun.   **87. Ismaros** (is′mä·ros).   **89. talents:** coins used in ancient
Greece; gold talents were of great value.   **111. whey** (hwā): the watery
part of milk. In cheese-making, whey is separated from the *curd,* or
thick part.

'Why not
take these cheeses, get them stowed, come back,
115   throw open all the pens, and make a run for it?
We'll drive the kids and lambs aboard. We say
put out again on good salt water!'
                                                    Ah,
how sound that was! Yet I refused. I wished
to see the caveman, what he had to offer—
120   no pretty sight, it turned out for my friends.

We lit a fire, burnt an offering,°
and took some cheese to eat; then sat in silence
around the embers, waiting. When he came
he had a load of dry boughs on his shoulder
125   to stoke his fire at suppertime. He dumped it
with a great crash into that hollow cave,
and we all scattered fast to the far wall.
Then over the broad cavern floor he ushered
the ewes he meant to milk. He left his rams
130   and he-goats in the yard outside, and swung
high overhead a slab of solid rock
to close the cave. Two dozen four-wheeled wagons,
with heaving wagon teams, could not have stirred
the tonnage of that rock from where he wedged it
135   over the doorsill. Next he took his seat
and milked his bleating ewes. A practiced job
he made of it, giving each ewe her suckling;°
thickened his milk, then, into curds and whey,
sieved out the curds to drip in withy° baskets,
140   and poured the whey to stand in bowls
cooling until he drank it for his supper.
When all these chores were done, he poked the fire,
heaping on brushwood. In the glare he saw us.

'Strangers,' he said, 'who are you? and where from?
145   What brings you here by sea ways—a fair traffic?°

---

121. **offering:** a sacrifice to the gods or a god.   137. **suckling:** *here,* a
baby lamb.   139. **withy:** flexible twigs (usually willow) woven together.   145. **a fair traffic:** lawful trade.

Or are you wandering rogues, who cast your lives
like dice, and ravage other folk by sea?'

We felt a pressure on our hearts, in dread
of that deep rumble and that mighty man.
150 But all the same I spoke up in reply:
'We are from Troy, Akhaians,° blown off course
by shifting gales on the Great South Sea;
homeward bound, but taking routes and ways
uncommon; so the will of Zeus° would have it.
155 We served under Agamemnon,° son of Atreus°—
the whole world knows what city°
he laid waste, what armies he destroyed.
It was our luck to come here; here we stand
beholden for your help, or any gifts
160 you give—as custom is to honor strangers.°
We would entreat you, great Sir, have a care
for the gods' courtesy; Zeus will avenge
the unoffending guest.'
                              He answered this
from his brute chest, unmoved:
                              'You are a ninny,
165 or else you come from the other end of nowhere,
telling me, mind the gods! We Cyclopes
care not a whistle for your thundering Zeus°
or all the gods in bliss; we have more force by far.
I would not let you go for fear of Zeus—
170 you or your friends—unless I had a whim to.
Tell me, where was it, now, you left your ship—
around the point, or down the shore, I wonder?'

He thought he'd find out, but I saw through this,
and answered with a ready lie:

---

151. Akhaians (ə·kē′ənz): Greeks; also spelled Achaeans. **154. Zeus**
(zōōs): king of the gods and ruler of heaven and earth. **155. Agamemnon** (ag′ə·mem′non): the king who led the Greek forces in the
Trojan War; **Atreus** (a′trē·əs). **156. what city:** Troy. **160. custom
is to honor strangers:** The Greeks believed that it was their duty to
help peaceful strangers. They believed that the gods sent wanderers and
beggars to test them. **167. thundering Zeus:** The symbol of Zeus's
power was a thunderbolt.

'My ship?
175 Poseidon Lord, who sets the earth a-tremble,°
broke it up on the rocks at your land's end.
A wind from seaward served him, drove us there.
We are survivors, these good men and I.'
Neither reply nor pity came from him,
180 but in one stride he clutched at my companions
and caught two in his hands like squirming puppies
to beat their brains out, spattering the floor.
Then he dismembered them and made his meal,
gaping and crunching like a mountain lion—
185 everything: innards, flesh, and marrow bones.
We cried aloud, lifting our hands to Zeus,
powerless, looking on at this, appalled;
but Cyclops went on filling up his belly
with manflesh and great gulps of whey,
190 then lay down like a mast° among his sheep.
My heart beat high now at the chance of action,
and drawing the sharp sword from my hip I went
along his flank to stab him where the midriff
holds the liver. I had touched° the spot
195 when sudden fear stayed me: if I killed him
we perished there as well, for we could never
move his ponderous doorway slab aside.
So we were left to groan and wait for morning.

When the young Dawn with finger tips of rose
200 lit up the world, the Cyclops built a fire
and milked his handsome ewes, all in due order,
putting the sucklings to the mothers. Then,
his chores being all dispatched, he caught
another brace° of men to make his breakfast,
205 and whisked away his great door slab
to let his sheep go through—but he, behind,
reset the stone as one would cap a quiver.°

175. Poseidon (pō·sī′dən) . . . **a-tremble:** Besides being god of the sea, Poseidon was god of earthquakes; he was commonly called the "earth-shaker." **190. like a mast:** as straight and tall as a ship's mast. **194. had touched:** almost touched. **204. brace:** a pair; the term is usually used when describing a catch of birds or game. **207. quiver:** a case in which arrows are carried.

There was a din of whistling as the Cyclops
rounded his flock to higher ground, then stillness.
210   And now I pondered how to hurt him worst,
if but Athena° granted what I prayed for.
Here are the means I thought would serve my turn:

a club, or staff, lay there along the fold—
an olive tree, felled green and left to season
215   for Cyclops' hand. And it was like a mast
a lugger of twenty oars, broad in the beam—
a deep-sea-going craft—might carry:
so long, so big around, it seemed. Now I
chopped out a six foot section of this pole
220   and set it down before my men, who scraped it;
and when they had it smooth, I hewed again
to make a stake with pointed end. I held this
in the fire's heart and turned it, toughening it,
then hid it, well back in the cavern, under
225   one of the dung piles in profusion there.
Now came the time to toss for it: who ventured
along with me? whose hand could bear to thrust
and grind that spike in Cyclops' eye, when mild
sleep had mastered him? As luck would have it,
230   the men I would have chosen won the toss—
four strong men, and I made five as captain.

At evening came the shepherd with his flock,
his woolly flock. The rams as well, this time,
entered the cave: by some sheep-herding whim—
235   or a god's bidding—none were left outside.
He hefted his great boulder into place
and sat him down to milk the bleating ewes
in proper order, put the lambs to suck,
and swiftly ran through all his evening chores.
240   Then he caught two more men and feasted on them.
My moment was at hand, and I went forward
holding an ivy bowl of my dark drink,
looking up, saying:

211. Athena (ə·thē′nə): Greek goddess of wisdom.

'Cyclops, try some wine.
Here's liquor to wash down your scraps of men.
245 Taste it, and see the kind of drink we carried
under our planks. I meant it for an offering
if you would help us home. But you are mad,
unbearable, a bloody monster! After this,
will any other traveller come to see you?'

250 He seized and drained the bowl, and it went down
so fiery and smooth he called for more:
'Give me another, thank you kindly. Tell me,
how are you called? I'll make a gift will please you.
Even Cyclopes know the wine-grapes grow
255 out of grassland and loam° in heaven's rain,
but here's a bit of nectar and ambrosia!'°

Three bowls I brought him, and he poured them down.
I saw the fuddle and flush come over him,
then I sang out in cordial tones:
'Cyclops,
260 you ask my honorable name? Remember
the gift you promised me, and I shall tell you.
My name is Nohbdy:° mother, father, and friends,
everyone calls me Nohbdy.'
And he said:
'Nohbdy's my meat, then, after I eat his friends.
265 Others come first. There's a noble gift, now.'
Even as he spoke, he reeled and tumbled backward,
his great head lolling to one side; and sleep
took him like any creature. Drunk, hiccuping,
he dribbled streams of liquor and bits of men.

270 Now, by the gods, I drove my big hand spike
deep in the embers, charring it again,
and cheered my men along with battle talk
to keep their courage up: no quitting now.

255. loam: a type of soil consisting of clay, sand, and silt. **256. nectar
and ambrosia:** Nectar was the liquid the gods drank; ambrosia was the
food they ate. Cyclops is saying that the wine is like food of the gods.
262. Nohbdy: Nobody.

The pike of olive, green though it had been,
275 reddened and glowed as if about to catch.
I drew it from the coals and my four fellows
gave me a hand, lugging it near the Cyclops
as more than natural force nerved them; straight
forward they sprinted, lifted it, and rammed it
280 deep in his crater eye,° and I leaned on it
turning it as a shipwright turns a drill
in planking, having men below to swing
the two-handled strap that spins it in the groove.
So with our brand° we bore that great eye socket
285 while blood ran out around the red hot bar.
Eyelid and lash were seared; the pierced ball
hissed broiling, and the roots popped.
                              In a smithy
one sees a white-hot axehead or an adze°
plunged and wrung in a cold tub, screeching steam—
290 the way they make soft iron hale and hard—:
just so that eyeball hissed around the spike.
The Cyclops bellowed and the rock roared around him,
and we fell back in fear. Clawing his face
he tugged the bloody spike out of his eye,
295 threw it away, and his wild hands went groping;
then he set up a howl for Cyclopes
who lived in caves on windy peaks nearby.
Some heard him; and they came by divers° ways
to clump around outside and call:
                              'What ails you,
300 Polyphemos? Why do you cry so sore
in the starry night? You will not let us sleep.
Sure no man's driving off your flock? No man
has tricked you, ruined you?'
                              Out of the cave
the mammoth Polyphemos roared in answer:
305 'Nohbdy, Nohbdy's tricked me, Nohbdy's ruined me!'
To this rough shout they made a sage reply:
'Ah well, if nobody has played you foul

---

280. crater eye: Cyclops' one eye was large and deep.   **284. brand:** *here,*
a burning piece of wood.   **288. adze** (adz): a carpenter's tool.
298. divers: various.

there in your lonely bed, we are no use in pain
given by great Zeus. Let it be your father,
Poseidon Lord, to whom you pray.'

310
                                          So saying
they trailed away. And I was filled with laughter
to see how like a charm the name deceived them.
Now Cyclops, wheezing as the pain came on him,
fumbled to wrench away the great doorstone

315
and squatted in the breach with arms thrown wide
for any silly beast or man who bolted—
hoping somehow I might be such a fool.
But I kept thinking how to win the game:
death sat there huge; how could we slip away?

320
I drew on all my wits, and ran through tactics,
reasoning as a man will for dear life,
until a trick came—and it pleased me well.
The Cyclops' rams were handsome, fat, with heavy
fleeces, a dark violet.
                                 Three abreast

325
I tied them silently together, twining
cords of willow from the ogre's bed;
then slung a man under each middle one
to ride there safely, shielded left and right.
So three sheep could convey each man. I took

330
the woolliest ram, the choicest of the flock,
and hung myself under his kinky belly,
pulled up tight, with fingers twisted deep
in sheepskin ringlets for an iron grip.
So, breathing hard, we waited until morning.

335
When Dawn spread out her finger tips of rose
the rams began to stir, moving for pasture,
and peals of bleating echoed round the pens
where dams with udders full called for a milking.
Blinded, and sick with pain from his head wound,

340
the master stroked each ram, then let it pass,
but my men riding on the pectoral fleece°
the giant's blind hands blundering never found.
Last of them all my ram, the leader, came,

341. **pectoral fleece:** wool of the chest.

weighted by wool and me with my meditations.
345   The Cyclops patted him, and then he said:

'Sweet cousin ram, why lag behind the rest
in the night cave? You never linger so,
but graze before them all, and go afar
to crop sweet grass, and take your stately way
350   leading along the streams, until at evening
you run to be the first one in the fold.
Why, now, so far behind? Can you be grieving
over your Master's eye? That carrion° rogue
and his accurst companions burnt it out
355   when he had conquered all my wits with wine.
Nohbdy will not get out alive, I swear.
Oh, had you brain and voice to tell
where he may be now, dodging all my fury!
Bashed by this hand and bashed on this rock wall
360   his brains would strew the floor, and I should have
rest from the outrage Nohbdy worked upon me.'
He sent us into the open, then. Close by,
I dropped and rolled clear of the ram's belly,
going this way and that to untie the men.
365   With many glances back, we rounded up
his fat, stiff-legged sheep to take aboard,
and drove them down to where the good ship lay.
We saw, as we came near, our fellows' faces
shining; then we saw them turn to grief
370   tallying those who had not fled from death.
I hushed them, jerking head and eyebrows up,
and in a low voice told them: 'Load this herd;
move fast, and put the ship's head toward the breakers.'
They all pitched in at loading, then embarked
375   and struck their oars into the sea.

353. carrion: dead flesh in the process of decaying; *here,* rotten, disgusting.

Meaning and Method

1. Before Odysseus enters the country of the Cyclopes, he feels
that he will meet some brute "all outward power,/a wild man,

ignorant of civility" (lines 102–103). How does the Cyclopes' way of life differ from Odysseus' more civilized view? Refer to lines 44–55 and 164–170 to find support for your answer.

2. What words or phrases in lines 74–80 and 129–136 convey a sense of the monstrous size and strength of Cyclops? What visual images in lines 179–190 make him appear a horrifying beast?

3. Odysseus says in line 2 that he is "formidable for guile." What tricks does he play on Cyclops that show his cunning? What did he gain, for example, by telling the giant that his name was "nohbdy"?

(*As Odysseus is leaving, he cannot resist taunting Cyclops, who finally throws an enormous rock at the ship, but does not hit it.*

(*Odysseus' next stop is the island of Aeolus, king of the winds. Aeolus gives Odysseus a bag containing the storm winds so that he will not be disturbed on his trip. However, as Odysseus' ship approaches Ithaca, his sailors, thinking the bag contains treasure, open it. The ship is blown back to the island of Aeolus, where the king tells Odysseus that he is obviously cursed by the gods and refuses to help him again.*

(*Odysseus and his crew sail next to the land of the man-eating Laestrygones, where they lose a number of men. The survivors escape, set sail again, and land on the island of Circe. Circe is a sorceress who turns some of Odysseus' men into swine, but Odysseus, with the gods' help, eventually gets her to turn the men back to human form. He and his shipmates then spend a year on the island, and are treated royally by Circe. When they leave, they visit the land of the dead, and then return to Circe, who gives the following prophecy.*)

CIRCE'S WARNING

'Listen with care
to this, now, and a god will arm your mind.
Square in your ship's path are Sirens, crying
beauty to bewitch men coasting by;
380   woe to the innocent who hears that sound!
He will not see his lady nor his children
in joy, crowding about him, home from sea;
the Sirens will sing his mind away

385 on their sweet meadow lolling. There are bones
of dead men rotting in a pile beside them
and flayed skins shrivel around the spot.

Steer wide;
keep well to seaward; plug your oarsmen's ears
with beeswax kneaded soft; none of the rest
should hear that song.

But if you wish to listen,
390 let the men tie you in the lugger, hand
and foot, back to the mast, lashed to the mast,
so you may hear those harpies'° thrilling voices;
shout as you will, begging to be untied,
your crew must only twist more line around you
395 and keep their stroke up, till the singers fade.

(*Circe next describes two possible courses Odysseus can take. One,
by way of the Prowling Rocks, or Drifters, is exceptionally dangerous.
Circe tells Odysseus that only one ship has ever made it safely past the
rocks, and its captain was helped by Hera, wife of Zeus. This course is
therefore effectively ruled out. She then describes the other course.*)

'A second course
lies between headlands. One is a sharp mountain
piercing the sky, with stormcloud round the peak
dissolving never, not in the brightest summer,
400 to show heaven's azure there, nor in the fall.
No mortal man could scale it, nor so much
as land there, not with twenty hands and feet,
so sheer the cliffs are—as of polished stone.
Midway that height, a cavern full of mist
405 opens toward Erebos° and evening. Skirting
this in the lugger, great Odysseus,
your master bowman, shooting from the deck,
would come short of the cavemouth with his shaft;

---

392. harpies: The harpies, like the Sirens, were part woman, part bird,
but unlike the Sirens, they were ugly monsters. Their victims were
chosen by the gods. Circe here uses the term to indicate that the effect of
the Sirens and the harpies was the same. **405. Erebos** (er'ə·bəs): the
entrance to Hades (hā'dēz), the land of the dead in Greek mythology. It
is named after the son of Chaos and signifies darkness.

but that is the den of Scylla,° where she yaps
410 abominably, a newborn whelp's cry,
though she is huge and monstrous. God or man,
no one could look on her in joy. Her legs—
and there are twelve—are like great tentacles,
unjointed, and upon her serpent necks
415 are borne six heads like nightmares of ferocity,
with triple serried° rows of fangs and deep
gullets of black death. Half her length, she sways
her heads in air, outside her horrid cleft,
hunting the sea around that promontory
420 for dolphins, dogfish, or what bigger game
thundering Amphitrite° feeds in thousands.
And no ship's company can claim
to have passed her without loss and grief; she takes,
from every ship, one man for every gullet.

425 The opposite point seems more a tongue of land
you'd touch with a good bowshot, at the narrows.
A great wild fig, a shaggy mass of leaves,
grows on it, and Charybdis lurks below
to swallow down the dark sea tide. Three times
430 from dawn to dusk she spews it up
and sucks it down again three times, a whirling
maelstrom;° if you come upon her then
the god who makes earth tremble could not save you.
No, hug the cliff of Scylla,° take your ship
435 through on a racing stroke. Better to mourn
six men than lose them all, and the ship, too.'
So her advice ran; but I faced her, saying:

'Only instruct me, goddess, if you will,
how, if possible, can I pass Charybdis,

---

409. Scylla: a once-beautiful nymph whom Poseidon had loved. Poseidon's jealous wife Amphitrite (am'fɔ·trīt'ē), goddess of the sea, had changed her to a monster. **416. serried:** ranked. **421. thundering Amphitrite:** The goddess of the sea was especially tempestuous when near Scylla. **432. maelstrom** (māl'strɔm): a whirlpool which violently sucks in objects. **428–434. Charybdis . . . Scylla:** If one has to choose between two evils, one is often said to be between Scylla and Charybdis.

440   or fight off Scylla when she raids my crew?'
Swiftly that loveliest goddess answered me:

'Must you have battle in your heart forever?
The bloody toil of combat? Old contender,
will you not yield to the immortal gods?
445   That nightmare cannot die, being eternal
evil itself—horror, and pain, and chaos;
there is no fighting her, no power can fight her,
all that avails is flight.
                Lose headway there
along that rockface while you break out arms,
450   and she'll swoop over you, I fear, once more,
taking one man again for every gullet.
No, no, put all your backs into it, row on;
invoke Blind Force, that bore this scourge° of men,
to keep her from a second strike against you.

455   Then you will coast Thrinakia,° the island
where Helios'° cattle graze, fine herds, and flocks
of goodly sheep. The herds and flocks are seven,
with fifty beasts in each.
                   No lambs are dropped,°
or calves, and these fat cattle never die.
460   Immortal, too, their cowherds are—their shepherds—
Phaëthousa° and Lampetia,° sweetly braided
nymphs that divine Neaira° bore
to the overlord of high noon, Helios.
These nymphs their gentle mother bred and placed
465   upon Thrinakia, the distant land,
in care of flocks and cattle for their father.

Now give those kine° a wide berth, keep your thoughts
intent upon your course for home,
and hard seafaring brings you all to Ithaca.

453. scourge (skûrj): one who inflicts severe punishment.
455. Thrinakia (thri·nā′kē·ə). **456. Helios** (hē′lē·ōs): another
name for Apollo in his role as god of the sun. **458. dropped:** born.
461. Phaëthousa (fā·thōō′sə); **Lampetia** (lam·pē′shə). **462. Neaira**
(nē·ē′rə). **467. kine** (kīn): cows.

470   But if you raid the beeves,° I see destruction
for ship and crew.
                  Rough years then lie between
you and your homecoming, alone and old,
the one survivor, all companions lost.'

470. beeves: a plural of *beef.*

Meaning and Method

Of what dangers does Circe warn Odysseus? How does she suggest that he save himself and his men from each danger? In her warnings (lines 442–448 and 467–471) she indicates her own—and perhaps the ancient Greek—view of human limitations. What is her attitude toward evil? toward humans' capacity to destroy it?

(When Odysseus leaves Circe, he tells his sailors what she had said about the Sirens, gives them wax to put in their ears, and because he wants to hear the Sirens, orders them to tie him to the mast in accordance with Circe's instructions. As Circe predicted, when he hears the Sirens sing, Odysseus orders the men to untie him, but they cannot hear him. Finally they pass the Sirens. Odysseus continues.)

SCYLLA AND CHARYBDIS

                          My faithful company
475   rested on their oars now, peeling off
the wax that I had laid thick on their ears;
then set me free.
                But scarcely had that island
faded in blue air than I saw smoke
and white water, with sound of waves in tumult—
480   a sound the men heard, and it terrified them.
Oars flew from their hands; the blades went knocking
wild alongside till the ship lost way,
with no oarblades to drive her through the water.

Well, I walked up and down from bow to stern,
485 trying to put heart into them, standing over
every oarsman, saying gently,
                                'Friends,
have we never been in danger before this?
More fearsome, is it now, than when the Cyclops
penned us in his cave? What power he had!
490 Did I not keep my nerve, and use my wits
to find a way out for us?
                                Now I say
by hook or crook this peril too shall be
something that we remember.
                                Heads up, lads!
We must obey the orders as I give them.
495 Get the oarshafts in your hands, and lay back
hard on your benches; hit these breaking seas.
Zeus help us pull away before we founder.

You at the tiller, listen, and take in
all that I say—the rudders are your duty;
500 keep her out of the combers° and the smoke;
steer for that headland; watch the drift, or we
fetch up in the smother, and you drown us.'

That was all, and it brought them round to action.
But as I sent them on toward Scylla, I
505 told them nothing, as they could do nothing.
They would have dropped their oars again, in panic,
to roll for cover under the decking. Circe's
bidding against arms had slipped my mind,
so I tied on my cuirass° and took up
510 two heavy spears, then made my way along
to the foredeck—thinking to see her first from there,
the monster of the grey rock, harboring
torment for my friends. I strained my eyes
upon that cliffside veiled in cloud, but nowhere
515 could I catch sight of her.

---

500. combers: long, crested waves.   **509. cuirass** (kwĭ·răs′): a piece
of armor which covers the chest.

And all this time,
in travail, sobbing, gaining on the current,
we rowed into the straight—Scylla to port
and on our starboard beam Charybdis, dire
gorge of the salt sea tide. By heaven! when she
520 vomited, all the sea was like a cauldron
seething over intense fire, when the mixture
suddenly heaves and rises.
                              The shot spume
soared to the landside heights, and fell like rain.
But when she swallowed the sea water down
525 we saw the funnel of the maelstrom, heard
the rock bellowing all around, and dark
sand raged on the bottom far below.
My men all blanched° against the gloom, our eyes
were fixed upon that yawning mouth in fear
530 of being devoured.
                      Then Scylla made her strike,
Whisking six of my best men from the ship.
I happened to glance aft at ship and oarsmen
and caught sight of their arms and legs dangling
high overhead. Voices came down to me
535 in anguish, calling my name for the last time.

A man surfcasting on a point of rock
for bass or mackerel, whipping his long rod
to drop the sinker and the bait far out,
will hook a fish and rip it from the surface
540 to dangle wriggling through the air:
                                        so these
were borne aloft in spasms toward the cliff.

She ate them as they shrieked there, in her den,
in the dire grapple, reaching still for me—
and deathly pity ran me through
545 at that sight—far the worst I ever suffered,
questing the passes of the strange sea.
                                        We rowed on.

528. **blanched:** turned white.

The Rocks were now behind; Charybdis, too,
and Scylla dropped astern.
                              Then we were coasting
the noble island of the god, where grazed
550   those cattle with wide brows, and bounteous flocks
of Helios, lord of noon, who rides high heaven." °

551. who rides high heaven: Apollo was supposed to drive the chariot
of the sun across the sky each day. When he started his ride, it was
dawn, and when he finished, it was sunset.

Meaning and Method

1. In spite of the warning, Odysseus journeys on. What reason
   does he give for not telling his men of Circe's prediction (see
   lines 504–507)? How do his determination to continue and his
   decision not to tell his men everything help to emphasize the
   difference between Odysseus and his men?
2. What do Odysseus' desire to listen to the Sirens and the precau-
   tions he takes in being bound to the mast show about his character? In what other incident did Odysseus show these characteristics?
3. Odysseus' men obey without question or hesitation the orders
   he has given them. What does their reaction to him say about
   his qualities of leadership? Point out words or actions that prove
   Odysseus returns the loyalty and affection his men feel for him.
4. Epics make use of elaborate comparisons, such as the one found
   in lines 536–542. Why is the comparison appropriate? That is,
   in what ways is Scylla's seizure of the men like a fisherman's
   hauling in of fish?

(*Odysseus' men, disobeying their leader and ignoring Circe's warning, eat the cattle of the sun. As a result, when they leave, their ship is
wrecked. Odysseus alone survives by making a makeshift raft of the ship's
mast and keel. On this, he drifts to an island on which the nymph Calypso
lives. Calypso detains him for seven years, until Zeus orders her to give up
her hopes of marrying Odysseus and release him. She then provides Odysseus with a well-stocked raft, which, however, is wrecked by Poseidon, god
of the sea.*)

(After his raft is wrecked, Odysseus floats to the land of a friendly king, who entertains him and helps him finally to return to Ithaca. There he finds that his faithful wife, Penelope, is besieged by suitors who insist that she choose one of them as a husband. With the help of his son, Telemachus, Odysseus eventually kills the suitors, is reunited with Penelope, and regains his former position as ruler.)

Meaning and Method

1. One of the characteristics of epics is the use of *epithets,* descriptive words or phrases which are used repeatedly in a work, and which sometimes come to be used in place of the name of a person. In the *Odyssey,* one frequently used epithet to describe the Dawn is *with finger tips of rose.* Why is this epithet appropriate? What epithet describes Helios in line 551? Why is it appropriate?

2. Among the characteristics of epics are the following:
   a. a main character who is a great hero;
   b. a setting of vast dimensions;
   c. action consisting of deeds which require great—sometimes superhuman—courage;
   d. intervention of supernatural forces.
   Which of these characteristics appear in the selection from the *Odyssey* that you have just read? Give specific examples to support your answers.

3. The words and deeds of Odysseus show him as a great hero. What characteristics has Homer given Odysseus to make him seem human as well?

Language: Modern Meanings for Words from the *Odyssey*

Several words you have encountered in the *Odyssey* are used today figuratively. Their meanings draw from their associations with the epic. What figurative meanings are implied by the ways these words are used in the following sentences?

1. The fireman stood frozen on the ledge, caught between the *Scylla* of jumping seven stories to the pavement and the *Charybdis* of turning back to the flaming stairway.

2. The recent flight to Mars marked still another *odyssey* into space.

3. Few television viewers can escape the *siren song* of the advertising world.

Composition

1. Think of an incident in history—recent or otherwise—which strikes you as being of epic proportions. Write a paragraph summarizing or explaining the incident, and another paragraph telling why you have chosen it.

2. Scylla, the Sirens, and the Cyclopes may be said to be present symbolically in the modern world as well as in the world of the ancient Greeks. The monster Scylla, the symbol of eternal evil, may be reflected in the prejudice and hate which still exist in our world. The Sirens, partly beautiful women who are the symbols of sensual lures, may be reflected in our desire for material possessions. The Cyclopes, symbols of brute force, may be reflected in wars and in some mindless, ungovernable violence.

Choosing Scylla, the Sirens, or the Cyclopes as your focus, write a composition in which you illustrate the presence and effect of these symbolic characters in our world. Use specific examples to support your points.

A GLOSSARY OF LITERARY TERMS

Abstract and Concrete Terms: an abstract term refers to an idea or quality, such as *truth* or *sweetness*. Its opposite, a concrete term, refers to something real—something which can be touched or seen, such as *book* or *sky*.

Alliteration: the repetition of sounds, usually consonant sounds, but sometimes vowel sounds, at the beginnings of words in the same line or in successive lines. For example:

> O *w*ild *W*est *W*ind, thou *b*reath of Autumn's *b*eing
> —Percy Bysshe Shelley, "Ode to the West Wind"

Allusion: a reference to a presumably familiar person, object, place, or event, or to a literary, historical, artistic, mythological, or biblical passage or work which the writer expects will be known to his readers. For example, in John Keat's "Ode to a Nightingale," the following lines appear:

> Perhaps the selfsame song that found a path
> Through the sad heart of Ruth, when, sick for home,
> She stood in tears amid the alien corn . . .

These lines allude to the biblical Book of Ruth, which tells the story of a young widow who left her own country to follow her mother-in-law, Naomi, to Naomi's homeland. Readers who know the story of Ruth will understand that alien corn refers to the fields in Naomi's country—a foreign or alien land to Ruth—in which Ruth gathered corn, or grain, for food.

Anapest: see **Meter.**

Apostrophe: the direct address to a deceased or absent person as if that person were present, or to an animal or thing, or an abstract idea or quality as if it could understand you. Apostrophe is sometimes used with personification.

An example of apostrophe without personification is:

> Little Lamb, who made thee?
> —William Blake, "The Lamb"

An example of apostrophe with personification is:

> With how sad steps, O Moon, thou climb'st the skies,
> How silently, and with how wan a face!
> —Philip Sidney, "With How Sad Steps, O Moon"

Assonance: the repetition of vowel sounds followed by different consonants. These words may appear in the same line or in successive lines. For example:

> Not marble, nor the g*i*lded monuments
> Of pr*i*nces, shall outl*i*ve th*i*s powerful rhyme.
> —William Shakespeare, "Sonnet 55"

Atmosphere: a pervasive element or influence. For example, there can be an atmosphere of melancholy, of gaiety, and so forth.

Ballad: a relatively short poem which tells a story. There are two types of ballads, *folk ballads* and *literary ballads*. Folk ballads were meant to be sung; literary ballads were meant to be printed and read. (See the discussion of the ballad on pages 93–94.)

Ballad Stanza: the most common stanza—or grouping of lines—used in ballads. It is a *quatrain,* or four-line stanza, with the second and fourth lines rhyming (see **Rhyme**). Generally each quatrain has four stressed syllables in the first and third lines, and three stressed syllables in the second and fourth lines. For example:

> There LIVED a WIFE at USHer's WELL,
> And a WEALthy WIFE was SHE:
> She HAD three STOUT and STALwart SONS,
> And SENT them O'ER the SEA.
> —Anonymous, "The Wife of Usher's Well"

Blank Verse: unrhymed poetry, in which each line usually has ten syllables. Five of the syllables are stressed—generally the second, fourth, sixth, eighth, and tenth syllables. For example:

> But, SOFT! What LIGHT through YONder WINdow BREAKS?
> It IS the EAST, and JULiet IS the SUN!
> ARISE, fair SUN, and KILL the ENvious MOON
> Who IS alREADy SICK and PALE with GRIEF
> That THOU her MAID art FAR more FAIR than SHE.
> —William Shakespeare, *Romeo and Juliet*

This arrangement of stressed and unstressed syllables in a ten-syllable line is called *iambic pentameter* (see **Meter**).

Character: a person in a play, story, novel, or poem.

Characterization: the creation of a literary character by such methods as description of physical appearance, presentation of thoughts and actions, and dialogue.

Colloquial Speech: a manner of speaking that is characteristic of informal conversation.

Concrete Terms: see **Abstract and Concrete Terms.**

Conflict: the clash of opposing forces—for example, people, ideas, themes, ways of life, or contradictory impulses within an individual.

Connotation: an association or suggestion which a word calls to mind in addition to its literal meaning (see **Denotation**). For example, a tree is literally "a perennial woody plant having usually a single self-supporting trunk of considerable height, with branches and foliage growing at some distance above the ground," but the word may suggest, connotatively, shade, a specific tree, a texture and color, etc.

Context: for a word, the other words surrounding it and having an effect on its meaning or use. The same words may have a different meaning in different contexts. For example, compare the meaning of the word *love* in "I love candy," and in the following lines in "Sonnet 73" by Elizabeth Barrett Browning:

> I love thee to the depth and breadth and height
> My soul can reach. . . .

Couplet: two successive lines, usually rhymed, which form a single unit of verse. For example:

> I was angry with my foe.
> I told it not, my wrath did grow.
> —William Blake, "A Poison Tree"

Dactyl: see **Meter.**

Denotation: the literal or dictionary meaning or meanings of a word (see also **Connotation**).

Dialect: the characteristic or distinctive speech of a particular group or the inhabitants of a certain geographical region. Dialect differs markedly in pronunciation and colloquial expressions from the standard speech of a country.

Dramatic Monologue: a type of poem in which a speaker addresses a listener or listeners who do not speak. The speaker reveals his or her character by commenting on a crucial problem or conflict in his or her life.

Dramatic Poetry: poetry in which one or more characters speak to other characters who may or may not answer. The dramatic monologue is one type of dramatic poetry.

Elegy: a poem mourning the death of an individual. It is often also a melancholy meditation on the trials and griefs of life in general. It is one type of lyric poem (see **Lyric**).

End Rhyme: see **Rhyme.**

Epic: a long story-poem which relates the deeds of a heroic character, usually a national hero.

Fable: a brief story in prose or verse aimed at illustrating a truth or moral (see **Moral**). Many fables, such as those of the Greek slave Aesop, are *beast fables* in which the characters are animals with distinctly human characteristics.

Figurative Language: language that is not meant to be interpreted on a strict literal level because it would make no sense or little sense if it were.

Figure of Speech: a word or phrase which describes something in a way that is not literally true but may be meaningful in a deeper sense. The effect of a figure of speech on the reader is generally stronger than that produced by everyday language (see **Simile, Metaphor, Personification, Irony,** and **Symbol** for discussions of some types of figures of speech).

Foot: a unit used in measuring or *scanning* lines of poetry. Each foot usually contains at least one stressed syllable. In addition, it usually has one or two unstressed syllables (see **Meter**).

Free Verse: poetry that does not have a strict or fixed rhythmic pattern or equal line lengths, and which does not rhyme. For example:

When Lilacs last in the dooryard bloom'd,
And the great star early droop'd in the western sky in the night,
I mourn'd and yet shall mourn with ever-returning spring.
—Walt Whitman, "When Lilacs Last in the Dooryard Bloom'd"

Iamb: see **Meter.**

Iambic Pentameter: see **Meter.**

Image: a word or phrase which brings a picture to the reader's mind or appeals to his senses of sight, hearing, touch, taste, or smell. The collective term for images is *imagery.*

Internal Rhyme: see **Rhyme.**

Irony: a figure of speech in which the writer says something in such a way that the opposite meaning is implied. For example, in Shakespeare's play, *Julius Caesar,* Mark Antony repeatedly calls Brutus, one of the murderers of Caesar, an "honorable man." However, because Mark Antony gives examples to show that Brutus' justification for the murder—that Caesar was "ambitious" and wanted to become dictator—was false, it becomes clear that he is really saying that Brutus was *not* honorable.

Irony may be present in a situation as well as in words. For example, in the ballad "Johnnie Armstrong," the outlaw Johnnie Armstrong insists that his men dress in their best clothes because the king has asked to see them. Because the king's intention is to hang him and his men, Johnnie's concern with the luxurious details of his men's clothing is part of an ironic situation.

Light Verse: verse which is primarily humorous or entertaining.

Lyric: a poem whose sole purpose is the expression of an individual's emotion or attitude. It is usually short and musical (see **Elegy, Ode,** and **Sonnet** for some specific types of lyrics).

Metaphor: a figure of speech in which one thing is compared indirectly to another dissimilar thing, without the use of *like* or *as*. For example:

> I'll tell you how the sun rose—
> A ribbon at a time."
> —Emily Dickinson, "I'll Tell You How the Sun Rose"

Although Metaphors usually contain nouns (for example, "ribbon" in the above lines), they may also be expressed solely in the verb. For example:

> Clouds and exlipses *stain* both moon and sun
> —William Shakespeare, "No More Be Grieved"

Metaphors may appear in one line of verse only, or they may be extended through many lines. For example, the first four lines of Shakespeare's "Sonnet 73" contain an *extended metaphor* in which middle age is compared to late autumn:

> That time of year thou may'st in me behold
> When yellow leaves, or none, or few, do hang
> Upon those boughs which shake against the cold,
> Bare ruined choirs where late the sweet birds sang

Meter: an organized rhythmic pattern created by the repetition of the same foot, or group of stressed and unstressed syllables, throughout a poem. Among the common metrical feet are:
anapestic—two unstressed syllables followed by one stressed syllable, as in in·ter·VENE. A single anapestic foot is called an *anapest*.
dactylic—one stressed syllable followed by two unstressed syllables, as in HIS·to·ry. A single dactylic foot is called a *dactyl*.
iambic—one unstressed syllable followed by one stressed syllable, as in de·FEND. A single iambic foot is called an *iamb*. A frequently used combination of iambic feet is called *iambic pentameter,* in which each line consists of five iambic feet. For example:

> True EASE/in WRIT/ing COMES/from ART,/not CHANCE
> —Alexander Pope, "Essay on Criticism"

trochaic—one stressed syllable followed by one unstressed syllable, as in **ES**·say. A single trochaic foot is called a *trochee*.

Mood: the overall emotional atmosphere or feeling in a literary work.

Moral: an ethical or practical lesson, usually illustrated by a story.

Narrator: one who tells or narrates a story.

Narrative Poem: a poem which tells a story, whether briefly as in the ballad or at length as in the epic.

Ode: a lyric poem which is lofty and dignified in subject matter and style.

Onomatopoeia (on′ə·mat·ə·pē′ə): the use of words whose sounds imitate natural sounds. For example: *buzz, whirr, moo, hiss.*

Paradox: a self-contradictory statement which nevertheless reveals some truth. For example:

> Stone walls do not a prison make,
> Nor iron bars a cage.
> —Richard Lovelace, "To Althea, from Prison"

Parody: the conscious exaggerated imitation of a literary style or individual work with the intention of achieving humor through distortion.

Personification: a figure of speech in which the writer attributes human qualities to animals, inanimate objects, or ideas. For example:

> Pale Ocean in unquiet slumber lay,
> And the wild Winds flew round, sobbing in their dismay.
> —Percy Bysshe Shelley, "Adonais"

Personification is often used with apostrophe (see **Apostrophe**).

Poetic Inversion: words arranged in such a way that they reverse in some manner the normal word order of a sentence. Often inversion is used for the sake of a rhyme. For example:

> None from his darts can fly,
> I am sick, I must die.
> —Thomas Nashe, "Adieu, Farewell Earth's Bliss"

Point of View: the standpoint from which a literary work is written. The point of view may change the way the writer presents a subject. For example, if writing from the personal point of view, the author may present only details that personally affected the "I." If writing from the third person point of view, the author may present details of which the participants in an action may not be aware. The point of view of the speaker may or may not be that of the poet.

Quatrain: a four-line stanza (see **Stanza**).

Rhyme: the repetition of two or more words reasonably close to each other in which the last vowel sound and the last consonant sound are the same. Example: June—moon; sea—me; sleep—weep. If the rhyme occurs at the end of the line, it is called an *end rhyme*. For example:

> He hangs in shades the orange bright,
> Like golden lamps in a green night.
>
> —Andrew Marvell, "Bermudas"

If a rhyme occurs within a line, it is called an *internal rhyme*. For example:

> The ant and the mole sit both in a hole.
>
> —Ben Jonson, "The Masque of Queens"

Rhyme Scheme: the pattern in which end rhyme occurs throughout a stanza or an entire poem. Rhyme schemes are usually denoted by italicized letters of the alphabet. For example, if the first and third lines of a four-line stanza rhyme, we say that the rhyme scheme is *abac* (*a* represents the rhyming words, while *b* and *c* represent the words that do not rhyme). If there are two rhymes in a four-line stanza, the rhyme scheme is *abab,* and if all four lines rhyme, it is *aaaa.*

Rhythm: in poetry, the recurrence or repetition of stressed and unstressed syllables in a regular pattern or manner. When rhythm in poetry is so strictly patterned that it can be measured in feet (see **Foot**), it is called meter (see **Meter**).

Satire: the use of ridicule, sarcasm, wit, or irony in order to expose, set right, or destroy a vice or folly.

Scansion: the method of determining the meter of a poem. When one *scans* a line, one counts the number and determines the type of poetic feet in that line.

Setting: the physical background of a work.

Simile: a figure of speech in which the comparison between two unlike things is expressed directly, usually by means of *like* or *as.* Two examples are William Wordsworth's line, "I wandered lonely *as* a cloud," and Robert Burns's line, "O, my luve's *like* a red, red rose."

Sonnet: a lyric poem of fourteen lines usually written in rhymed iambic pentameter (see **Meter**). Sonnets usually follow one of two types of rhyme schemes, but the rhymes may vary.

Speaker: the person whose voice we "hear" in the poem. (Note that the use of *I* does not necessarily mean that the speaker is the poet.)

Stanza: a group of lines which constitute a division in a poem. There is space before the first line, and after the last line of each group. In most poems, each stanza contains the same number of lines.

Symbol: in a poem, generally a figure of speech in which an object, person, place, event, or quality is chosen to stand for something other than itself—something which is not directly compared in the poem. For example, the road is a symbol of movement through life in "Sixty-Eighth Birthday" by James Russell Lowell:

As life runs on, the road grows strange
With faces new, and near the end
The milestones into headstones change,
'Neath every one a friend.

Notice that although life is mentioned, the road is not described directly as the road of life, or compared to life by means of *like* or *as*.

Theme: the central idea or one of the main ideas underlying a literary work.

Tone: the poet's attitude toward the subject or audience. Tone in poetry corresponds to tone in speaking.

Trochee: see **Meter.**

Type: a character who embodies the characteristics of a group or class rather than a strong individual personality.

Verse: a work consisting of metrical or rhythmical lines made up of a specified number of feet (see **Meter**). Verse may also be used as a synonym for poetry.

THE LANGUAGE ARTS PROGRAM
LIST OF SKILLS

Throughout the text, language arts have been integrated with the presentation of literature. The majority of language arts activities appear in the end-of-selection questions and assignments under the headings **Meaning, Method, Language, Composition,** and **Composition and Discussion.** Others are introduced and discussed in the general introductions, and still others, especially those concerning word origins and derivations, are covered in text footnotes.

The following indexes are intended to serve as guidelines to specific aspects of the language arts program in *A Book of Poetry* 1.

Epithet, 265
Feet, 4
Figurative language, 3, 26, 31, 73, 158, 175, 265
Figures of speech, 3, 73
Free verse, 52, 181
Iambic meter, 4, 238
Imagery and images, 1, 9–10, 12, 14, 16, 21, 22, 28, 34, 36, 39, 52, 73, 118, 150, 160, 170, 173, 186, 201, 223, 257
Humor, 76, 80, 221, 264
Irony, 48, 182, 221, 234
Line length, 73
Lyric, 5, 148, 225
Metaphor, 3, 10, 12, 26, 28, 39, 82, 84, 133, 154, 162, 178, 189
Meter, 4–5, 100, 154, 169, 186, 189
Mood, 62, 113, 146, 151, 154, 170, 173, 177, 186, 189, 194, 198, 202, 203, 209, 220, 221
Mythology, 133, 142 fn., 146, 229 fn., 223 fn., 241–243
Narrative poetry, 5, 93, 225, 241
Narrator, 118, 133
Onomatopoeia, 55, 151, 170, 186, 198–199
Parody, 217
Personification, 3, 40, 42, 43, 44, 84, 127
Plot, 93
Point of View, 148, 216, 217, 219, 227
Refrain, 93
Repetition, 85, 88, 103, 117, 118, 146–147, 155, 156, 170, 175, 203, 220
Rhyme, 3–4, 76, 85, 93, 218
Rhyme scheme, 4, 76, 84, 100, 146, 189, 218, 222, 223
Rhythm, 4–5, 73, 111, 127, 154, 156, 186, 194, 228

Satire, 76
Scanning, 4
Setting, 16, 167, 175, 177, 193, 202, 203, 217, 225
Simile, 3, 9–10, 26, 29, 34, 133, 165, 209, 212
Sonnet, 64, 148
Speaker, 5, 28, 31, 34, 36, 42, 55, 59, 62, 64, 66, 68, 69, 73, 76, 82, 88, 98, 133, 137, 145, 146, 154, 162, 169, 170, 173, 175, 177, 181, 184, 186, 189, 191, 201, 203, 204, 209, 210, 211, 212, 214, 220, 221, 222, 223, 225
Stanza, 51, 69, 80, 177, 216, 218
Suspense, 66, 103, 117, 118
Symbol, 56–57, 59, 68, 71, 181, 184, 186, 216, 218, 222, 223, 231, 234, 238, 246
Theme, 93, 100, 111, 114, 127, 133, 181, 191, 223
Tone, 31, 64, 73, 76, 137, 154, 164
Trochaic meter, 4
Understatement, 193

VOCABULARY DEVELOPMENT

Language activities (in order of appearance in the text): How scientific and medical terms are formed, 76; Origin of names, 98; Dialects, 101; Origins of the English language, 103; Pronunciation and spelling, 107; Prefixes, 138; Allusions to mythology, 146; Onomatopoeic words, 151; Words and expressions from the Bible, 156; expressing abstract ideas in concrete terms, 178; Words

Writing Poetry

D
E 6
F 7
G 8
H 9
I 0
J 1